# T-SHIRT JAPANESE
## *versus*
# NECKTIE JAPANESE
## TWO LEVELS OF POLITENESS

# T-SHIRT JAPANESE
### *versus*
# NECKTIE JAPANESE
## TWO LEVELS OF POLITENESS

Hiroko Fukuda

Translated by
**Charles De Wolf**

KODANSHA INTERNATIONAL
Tokyo • New York • London

For Setsuko Majima

Distributed in the United States by Kodansha America, Inc., 114
Fifth Avenue, New York, N.Y. 10011 and in the United Kingdom
and continental Europe by Kodansha Europe Ltd., 95 Aldwych,
London WC2B 4JF. Published by Kodansha International Ltd.,
17-14 Otowa 1-chome, Bunkyo-ku, Tokyo 112 and
Kodansha America, Inc.

95 96 97 10 9 8 7 6 5 4 3 2 1

ISBN 4-7700-1834-7

# CONTENTS

Preface                                    6

Where Do I Change Trains?                 10

At the Airport                            26

Tied Up in a Meeting                      46

Exchanging Business Cards                 62

In the Dressing Room                      76

Parents and Children's Fitness Day        94

My Lovely/Birdbrained Wife               118

Straight Talk                            134

# PREFACE

One of the greatest challenges for learners of Japanese is mastering the various levels of politeness called for in a range of everyday situations. The study of levels of politeness in speech is basically the study of human relations. We go about our days adjusting our linguistic clothing to suit the occasion, and while we may put on a tuxedo or evening dress once in a while for the strictest of formal events, we get by mainly on a combination of business suits and a necktie or pumps for day; and T-shirt and other casual wear for cutting loose with friends.

This book approaches Japanese language learning from this point of view of comparing the relaxed speech style acceptable around those with whom one feels at home to the more proper forms required in the world of, for instance, business. Since these two politeness levels—which we are calling T-Shirt and Necktie—are the most commonly used in everyday life, they are the ones that students gain most from studying.

Needless to say, a great many factors—when? where? who? and how much politeness is correct—come into play in any split-second decision about which speech forms to choose at any given time. Of course, no language can be cleanly split into two separate levels. In fact, people generally—often naturally and sometimes deliberately—mix elements from the different levels. And yet I believe that this focus is one of the quickest routes in to the heart of the Japanese language, which is in its human relationships.

Many factors influence the choices that must constantly be made in the course of speaking Japanese, but surely one of the most influential is the dichotomy between a person's in-group (*uchi*) and out-group (*soto*). The in-group spans the members of one's family, school, company, home town or any other groups to which one feels a sense of belonging. The out-group comprises the opposite: anyone deemed to fall outside those groups. The various layers of the in-group, however, overlap and shift into and out of prominence regularly as one moves through a variety of different social situations. Still, taken as a whole, they form the background of social, geographic and psychological elements that are basic to a sense of identity.

Another extremely influential factor is the hierarchical framework of human relationships represented by the terms *me-ue* (social betters/superiors) and *me-shita* (underlings). The basic standards for determining people's relative standing within this framework are age and social position. The fact, for instance, that students speak in a respectful language style to teachers, and that teachers use casual language in return, is related to differences in both their ages and relative social position. The teachings of Confucius have for centuries helped to shape this way of thinking.

Japanese is intrinsically a language of relationship. Any "I" that people refer to in Japan is likely to be located squarely within some established social organization or framework. The Japanese language makes very little provision for an isolated or, we might say, independent self.

By all means, do bear these factors in mind as "key phrases" as you continue to grapple with the Japanese language; often they can help interpret some of the otherwise mystifying things you may notice about Japan. I hope that you will refrain from making snap judgments about the country or its people, and simply allow the patterns of human relationships to emerge gradually. Most of all I hope that this book may be of help in this way, throwing a new light on the faces of your friends, bringing out details you may never have noticed before.

**Acknowledgments:** A great many people helped, in tangible and intangible ways, to bring this book into being. I am not able to thank every one of them individually here, but I am grateful to each.

I would like to take this opportunity to thank, first of all, the small group of people who worked tirelessly to produce this book: my editors Shigeyoshi Suzuki of the Editorial Department of Kodansha International and Elizabeth Floyd; linguist Charles De Wolf, who translated my text; and *Power Japanese* editor Michael Brase. I was very impressed with their dedication to their work and their love of language, and remain deeply grateful.

I would also like to thank Tom Gally who provided invaluable advice in the planning stages and all my friends in Europe who asked me, throughout the process, when on earth this book would actually be finished.

Finally, I must thank the late Setsuko Majima. I will never forget the passion and vitality she poured into her teaching of Japanese.

# How to Use This Book

Each chapter contains a T-Shirt and a Necktie **dialogue.** Their content is basically the same, but is slightly altered, in both Japanese and the English translation, to reflect the different levels of politeness. You can read the two dialogues together to compare them, or just focus on the politeness level in which you are most interested. Feel free to use the dialogues in whatever way seems the most useful to you.

The **sample sentences** are phrased in natural spoken Japanese and strike a good balance between men's and women's speech. The various forms of shorthand used in the sample sentences are:

TJ  T-Shirt Japanese (informal expressions)
NJ  Necktie Japanese (formal expressions)
M  Masculine language
F  Feminine language

**Japanese punctuation** consists basically of the *tōten* (、 ) and the *kuten* (。 ), which are very similar in function to the comma and period respectively. In cases in which only intonation would clarify that a sentence is a question, a question mark has been substituted for the *kuten.*

An **Equivalency Chart** appears at the end of each chapter listing the key phrases from the T-Shirt and Necktie dialogues side-by-side for ease of comparison. You may want to refer to this to check on what has changed from one dialogue to another. The various codes used within the Equivalency Chart are:

—  Shows that no words are said (usually in T-Shirt)
~  Shows the location where the same words appear in the T-Shirt and Necktie dialogues

Many **cross-references** appear throughout the text where appropriate.

The **phrases** in the dialogue that appear in boldface are key phrases that change slightly from the TJ to the NJ dialogues.

# Where Do I Change Trains?

## 乗り換え駅は?

## T-SHIRT JAPANESE

Stephanie Dentzer and her friend Hiroko are at Akasaka-mitsuke. Stephanie is going on alone to Kamiyacho. Looking at the subway map, she asks Hiroko for some help.

**Stephanie:** Hey, could I ask you something? How do I get to Kamiyacho from here?

**Hiroko:** Kamiyacho? Let's see … You'd take the Marunouchi Line and transfer at Kasumigaseki to the Hibiya Line.

**Stephanie:** Huh? At *Kasumi* …?

**Hiroko:** Kasumigaseki. You get the Marunouchi Line going toward Ikebukuro. It's two stops from there.

**Stephanie:** And from Kasumigaseki I get the Hibiya Line, right?

**Hiroko:** Right. It's just one stop from there.

**Stephanie:** Okay, thanks.

## Tシャツ

ステファニー　**あのう、ちょっと聞きたいんだけど。神谷町へはどう行けばいいのかしら。**

浩子　　　神谷町？ええっと……。丸の内線に乗って、霞ヶ関で日比谷線に乗り換えよ。

ステファニー　えっ？カスミ……。

浩子　　　　カスミガセキ。丸の内線の池袋行きで、ここ
　　　　　　からふたつめ。

ステファニー　カスミガセキからは日比谷線ね。

浩子　　　　うん、そう。そこからひと駅よ。

ステファニー　ありがとう。


# T-SHATSU

**Sutefanii:** *Anō, chotto **kikitai n' da kedo**. Kamiyachō e wa dō ikeba ii **no kashira**.*

**Hiroko:** *Kamiyachō? Eetto ... Marunouchi-sen ni notte, Kasumigaseki de Hibiya-sen ni norikae **yo**.*

**Sutefanii:** *E'? Kasumi ...*

**Hiroko:** *Kasumigaseki. Marunouchi-sen no Ikebukuro-yuki de, koko kara futatsume.*

**Sutefanii:** *Kasumigaseki kara wa Hibiya-sen **ne**.*

**Hiroko:** *Un, sō. Soko kara hitoeki **yo**.*

**Sutefanii:** *Arigatō.*


| T-SHIRT NOTES |
| --- |

## • All-purpose *anō*

*Anō* is a lengthened version of *ano* ("that," "those," "over there") and functions as a different kind of "pointer." You can use it to get a person's attention, whether you want to start a conversation or emphasize the next point you will make.

*Anō* also comes in handy as "filler" thrown in when you are not sure how to frame your thoughts and are groping for the right words. It is appropriate too when you plan to broach a difficult topic and want to give your listener some advance warning. *Anō* often appears at the beginning of sentences, but can also be sandwiched between phrases. *Anō* is used in both T-Shirt and Necktie Japanese.

あなた覚えてる？ あのう、このあいだ行ったおいしいおそば
やさん。(TJ/F)

*Anata oboete 'ru? Anō, kono aida itta oishii osobaya-san.*

Say, do you remember that—you know—that delicious noo-dle shop we went to the other day?

あのう、ちょっとおたずねしますが、この辺に交番はないで
しょうか？(NJ/MF)

*Anō, chotto otazune shimasu ga, kono hen ni kōban wa nai deshō ka?*

Excuse me, could you tell me if there's a police box near here?

あのう、大変申し上げにくいことなんですが、私どもも迷惑
しているんです。(NJ/MF)

*Anō, taihen mōshiage-nikui koto nan desu ga, watakushi-domo mo meiwaku shite iru n' desu.*

I really hate to say this, but this is something that has been bothering us.

それで、あのう、冷蔵庫のお支払いの件なんですが、分割払
いにしていただけないでしょうか？(NJ/MF)

*Sore de, anō, reizōko no oshiharai no ken nan desu ga, bun-katsu-barai ni shite itadakenai deshō ka?*

Would it be possible for me to, uh, pay for the refrigerator by installment?

• *Chotto*: when "little" means a lot

*Chotto* is an adverb meaning "somewhat" or "just a little." But it's also often used to suggest that what is being discussed is so unim-portant and minor it's hardly worth mentioning. It functions as a "softener," cushioning the impact of what you say. With *chotto*, you can avoid coming across as high-handed, or indicate that you are about to request some tiny favor or interrupt in some small way. The word also provides a convenient hedge when you want to avoid giving a reply and yet don't want to sound rude.

ちょっとどいてよ。(TJ/MF)
*Chotto doite yo.*
Hey, move (over), will you?

これが終わったらちょっとお茶でも飲みに行かない？ (TJ/MF)
*Kore ga owattara **chotto** ocha de mo nomi ni ikanai?*
How about going out for a cup of coffee or something when we're finished here?

ちょっとご相談に乗っていただきたいことがあるんですが、よろしいでしょうか？(NJ/MF)
***Chotto** gosōdan ni notte itadakitai koto ga aru n' desu ga, yoroshii deshō ka?*
There's something I'd like to talk with you about, if I may.

ゆうべ遅くまで何してたの？(TJ/F)
*Yūbe osoku made nani shite 'ta no?*
What were you up to, till so late last night?
うん、ちょっとね。(TJ/MF)
*Un, **chotto** ne.*
Well, uh …

ちょっと行ってくる。夕飯までには帰るよ。(TJ/M)
***Chotto** itte kuru. Yūhan made ni wa kaeru yo.*
I'm going out for a while. I'll be back by suppertime.

• **Masculine and feminine language in T-Shirt Japanese**

Differences in the way men and women speak are particularly noticeable in T-Shirt language. Some interjections, and some particles added to the ends of sentences to achieve a certain nuance, are common to both sexes, while others are used exclusively by one or the other. For instance, both genders make use of the emphatic *sa*, while women are normally the only ones to use *kashira*. To take a look at some of the contrasts:

| FEMININE | MASCULINE |
|---|---|
| どう行けばいいのかしら。 | どう行けばいいのかなあ。 |
| *Dō ikeba ii no **kashira**.* | *Dō ikeba ii no **ka nā**.* |
| I wonder what's the best way to get there. | |

| | |
|---|---|
| 霞ヶ関からは日比谷線ね。 | 霞ヶ関からは日比谷線だね。 |
| *Kasumigaseki kara wa* | *Kasumigaseki kara wa* |
| *Hibiya-sen **ne**.* | *Hibiya-sen **da ne**.* |
| From Kasumigaseki, I get the Hibiya Line, right? | |

そこからひと駅よ。　　　　　　そこからひと駅だよ。
*Soko kara hitoeki **yo**.*　　　　*Soko kara hitoeki **da yo**.*
　　　　　　　　It's just one stop from there.

There is a growing tendency nowadays, especially among younger people, for women to use forms that were once masculine in tone. Depending on the context, however, this can give a woman's speech a "rough" edge, suggesting a lack of refinement.

Men, on the other hand, especially those who have learned their Japanese primarily from women teachers, should note that use of the so-called feminine forms is largely confined to homosexual men who wish to "camp it up" or give an impression of effeminacy.

### • *Kashira*

*Kashira* can be added to the end of women's T-Shirt sentences for any of the following five meanings. It is equivalent to men's *ka na* or *ka nā*.

(1) To express doubt, as if talking to oneself. This usage is often tinged with emotion, particularly a kind of casual admiration, or a certain sense of misgiving or concern.

かさを持って行かなくて大丈夫**かしら**。(TJ/F)
*Kasa o motte ikanakute daijōbu **kashira**.*
I don't really need an umbrella, do I?

頭が痛いわ。かぜでもひいたの**かしら**。(TJ/F)
*Atama ga itai wa. Kaze de mo hiita no **kashira**.*
I have such a headache. I wonder if I'm coming down with a cold.

(2) To ask a question.

マーケットは何時に開く**かしら**。(TJ/F)
*Māketto wa nanji ni aku **kashira**.*
What time does the market open?

このボールペン、あなたのじゃない**かしら**。(TJ/F)
*Kono bōru pen, anata no ja nai **kashira**.*
Would this be your pen?

(3) To give yourself a gentle prod or to solicit agreement from the listener.

> きょうの晩ごはんはてんぷらにしよう**かしら**。(TJ/F)
> *Kyō no bangohan wa tenpura ni shiyō kashira.*
> Let's see, maybe tempura would be good for supper tonight.

> そろそろ寝よう**かしら**。(TJ/F)
> *Sorosoro neyō kashira.*
> What do you say we go to bed now.

(4) When used with *nan to* or *nan te*, as an exclamation of surprise or admiration, similar to "How ~ !" or "What ~ !"

> 何といい天気なの**かしら**。(TJ/F)
> ***Nanto** ii tenki na no kashira.*
> Ah, what great weather!

> この犬、何てかわいいの**かしら**。(TJ/F)
> *Kono inu, **nante** kawaii no kashira.*
> What a cute dog!

(5) As in other languages, a negative construction (~ *nai kashira*) can express a positive wish.

> 早くバスが来ないかしら。(TJ/F)
> *Hayaku basu ga ko**nai kashira**.*
> Is there a bus soon, I wonder?

> 雨があがらないかしら。(TJ/F)
> *Ame ga agara**nai kashira**.*
> Isn't this rain ever going to let up?

### • *Eetto*: a clever device for catching your conversational breath

*Eetto*, a variant of *eeto*, can be used as a wind-up for your next verbal pitch. It gives you time to plan and signals to the listener that the ball is on its way. It fills a pause as you look at a subway map, open a pocket notebook to verify your schedule, or search your memory for a stray piece of information. Like *anō* (and the English "umm" or "er-r-r"), it allows you to "hold the floor" while thinking about what to say.

### • *Kosoado words*

The so-called *kosoado* words include *kō* ("this way"); *sō* ("that way"); *ā* ("that way"); and *dō* ("how"), as well as other groups of phrases that have *ko*, etc. as their first syllable.

In general, words that start with *ko-* indicate proximity to the speaker (*koko* "here"); *so-*, proximity to the listener (*soko* "there"); and *a-*, proximity to neither (*asoko* "over there"). *Do-* indicates uncertainty (*doko* "where").

As can be seen from the dialogues, however, this explanation alone does not fully account for actual usage. Why does Hiroko refer to Kasumigaseki as *soko* and not *asoko,* when the station is not close at hand for either her or Stephanie?

There are actually two possible answers to this question, to be found in two other important rules governing the use of *kosoado* words. One is that these words indicate how familiar the people talking are with the thing being discussed. If both people are familiar with the topic, it can be referred to as *asoko* ("there/that place we both know") or *ano* (e.g., *ano hito* "he/that guy/that person we both know or know of") or *are* (e.g., *rei no are* "that—you know—what we were talking about before"). But when at least one of the two people shows a lack of familiarity with the thing being discussed, it becomes *so*, as in *soko* ("there"), *sore* ("that"), *sono* (e.g., *sono hito* "that guy/he"), etc. Thus, in the dialogue, Hiroko uses *soko* because Stephanie has indicated that she is unfamiliar with the place.

Yet another explanation is possible. The first time a topic is introduced into a conversation, it might be, for instance, "Akasakamitsuke." In the times after that, though, it can become *soko* "there." In this case, *soko* functions like the English "the" or "that" (either of which can, of course, be used as soon as a specific topic has been narrowed down). This explanation would also apply in the dialogue.

# THE *KOSOADO* SYSTEM AT A GLANCE

| PART OF SPEECH | DISTANCE | | | |
|---|---|---|---|---|
| | close by (closer to speaker) | a short distance away (closer to listener) | further away (close to neither) | indeterminate |
| Personal Pronoun | この方<br>*kono kata*<br>この人<br>*kono hito*<br>こいつ<br>*koitsu*<br>this person | その方<br>*sono kata*<br>その人<br>*sono hito*<br>そいつ<br>*soitsu*<br>that person | あの方<br>*ano kata*<br>あの人<br>*ano hito*<br>あいつ<br>*aitsu*<br>that person | どの方<br>*dono kata*<br>どの人<br>*dono hito*<br>どいつ<br>*doitsu*<br>which person |
| Demonstrative Pronoun for things | これ<br>*kore*<br>this | それ<br>*sore*<br>that | あれ<br>*are*<br>that | どれ<br>*dore*<br>which |
| for places | ここ<br>*koko*<br>here | そこ<br>*soko*<br>there | あそこ<br>*asoko*<br>there | どこ<br>*doko*<br>where |
| for direction | こちら<br>*kochira*<br>こっち<br>*kotchi*<br>this way | そちら<br>*sochira*<br>そっち<br>*sotchi*<br>that way | あちら<br>*achira*<br>あっち<br>*atchi*<br>that way | どちら<br>*dochira*<br>どっち<br>*dotchi*<br>which way |
| "*Na*" adjective | こんな<br>*konna*<br>this kind of | そんな<br>*sonna*<br>that kind of | あんな<br>*anna*<br>that kind of | どんな<br>*donna*<br>what kind of |

| | | | | |
|---|---|---|---|---|
| Adjective | この<br>*kono*<br>this | その<br>*sono*<br>that<br>(over there) | あの<br>*ano*<br>that | どの<br>*dono*<br>what |
| Adverb | こう<br>*kō*<br>like this | そう<br>*sō*<br>like that | ああ<br>*ā*<br>like that | どう<br>*dō*<br>how; like what |

# NECKTIE JAPANESE

Stephanie Dentzer is looking at the subway map at Akasaka-mitsuke, trying to figure out how to get to Kamiyacho. Finally, she asks a woman passerby for help.

**Dentzer:** Pardon me. Could you tell me how to get to Kamiyacho?

**Woman:** Kamiyacho? Well, let's see … You would take the Marunouchi Line to Kasumigaseki and transfer there to the Hibiya Line.

**Dentzer:** I'm sorry. That station was *Kasumi* …?

**Woman:** *Kasumigaseki.* You'll be going in the direction of Ikebukuro, so it will be the second stop.

**Dentzer:** I see. And from Kasumigaseki I'll take the Hibiya Line, is that right?

**Woman:** That's right. You'll go just one stop on that line.

**Dentzer:** I see. Thank you very much.

## ネクタイ

| | |
|---|---|
| デンツァ | **すみません、ちょっとおたずねしたいんですが**……。神谷町へはどう行けばいいんでしょうか。 |
| 女性 | 神谷町**ですか**。ええっと……。丸の内線に乗って、霞ヶ関で日比谷線に乗り換え**ですね**。 |
| デンツァ | えっ？**すみません、**カスミ……。 |
| 女性 | カスミガセキ**です**。丸の内線の池袋行きで、ここからふたつめ**です**。 |
| デンツァ | カスミガセキからは日比谷線**ですね**。 |

女性　**ええ、そうです。** そこからひと駅です。

デンツァ　**どうもありがとうございました。**

# NEKUTAI

**Dentsā:** *Sumimasen, chotto otazune shitai n' desu ga ... Kamiyachō e wa dō ikeba ii n' deshō ka.*

**Josei:** *Kamiyachō desu ka. Eetto ... Marunouchi-sen ni notte, Kasumigaseki de Hibiya-sen ni norikae desu ne.*

**Dentsā:** *E'? Sumimasen, Kasumi ... ?*

**Josei:** *Kasumigaseki desu. Marunouchi-sen no Ikebukuro-yuki de, koko kara futatsume desu.*

**Dentsā:** *Kasumigaseki kara wa Hibiya-sen desu ne.*

**Josei:** *Ee, sō desu. Soko kara hitoeki desu.*

**Dentsā:** *Dōmo arigatō gozaimashita.*

---

| NECKTIE NOTES |

• **Using *sumimasen* to apologize or get someone's attention**

*Sumimasen* is primarily a polite expression used to express apologies or appreciation. It is also used simply to get another person's attention. So it is very much like the English "Excuse me ..." It is also used when you want someone to repeat a statement or question.

いつも君には苦労かけて**すまない**ね。(TJ/M)
*Itsumo kimi ni wa kurō o kakete sumanai ne.*
Sorry I'm always coming to you for things like this.

ご迷惑をおかけして、どうも**すみません**でした。(NJ/MF)
*Gomeiwaku o okake shite, dōmo sumimasen deshita.*
I'm sorry for putting you to all this trouble.

**すみません**。お待たせしました。(NJ/MF)

***Sumimasen***. *Omatase shimashita.*
Sorry to have kept you waiting. (Thank you for waiting.)

いつもいただいてばかりです**すみません**。(NJ/MF)
*Itsumo itadaite bakari de **sumimasen**.*
You've done far too much (for me) already.

**すみません**が、また今度にしていただけないでしょうか。
(NJ/MF)
***Sumimasen** ga, mata kondo ni shite itadakenai deshō ka.*
I'm sorry, but could we possibly put this off till another time?

**すみません**が、お塩をとっていただけますか。(NJ/MF)
***Sumimasen** ga, oshio o totte itadakemasu ka.*
Excuse me, could you pass the salt?

### • Set expressions used when introducing inquiries

When asking strangers questions, *sumimasen, chotto otazune shitai n' desu ga* is a handy phrase to remember. Other ways to say the same thing include *sumimasen, chotto otazune shimasu ga* and *sumimasen, chotto okiki shitai n' desu ga.*

すみません、**ちょっとおたずねしたいんですが**、駅はどこで
しょうか。(NJ/MF)
*Sumimasen, **chotto otazune shitai n' desu ga**, eki wa doko deshō ka.*
Excuse me, but could you tell me where the station is?

### • Use *desu* and *-masu* with your out-group

When talking to strangers or people you don't know very well, a good rule of thumb is to use the basic polite forms *desu* and *-masu.* In day-to-day conversation, there is no need for you to use the kind of humble expressions that bank employees or shops clerks use toward customers, or the heavily honorific phrases that you may sometimes hear, for instance, at formal gatherings, spoken by elderly women who are part of the social elite.

Nevertheless, in Japan, the use of what we might call "ordinary polite" forms (*desu/-masu*) even between long-standing acquaintances is taken simply as a sign of good breeding. The inappropriate use of T-Shirt Japanese can easily convey an impression of brusqueness or even rudeness.

## • E' for surprise

The abrupt *e'* (technically, *e* followed by a glottal stop) is a questioning response which is often interjected into conversation in one of two different ways.

*E'* can be used when you could not hear, or did not understand, what the other person said. Alternatively, it indicates surprise at the other person's remark. In either case, the inflection rises, questioningly, at the end. A light, clipped pronunciation suggests slight or casual questioning. When the word is stressed or drawn out, the implication is that you are a bit taken aback, or that you have trouble believing what the other person said.

(With a clipped pronunciation)
えっ、今何か言った？(TJ/MF)
*E', ima nani ka itta?*
Huh? Did you say something?

(With the *e'* more drawn out)
えっ、本当？そんなことちっとも知らなかったわ。(TJ/F)
*E', hontō? Sonna koto chitto mo shiranakatta wa.*
What? Re-e-e-ally? I had no idea!

## • The long *ee* of agreement

The long *ee* of agreement is used in both T-Shirt and Necktie Japanese, by both men and women. However, men tend to use it less in T-Shirt conversation than do women; the word lends an extra air of softness or gentleness that in women's casual speech is considered polite. Men often use it in more formal situations, in order to dispel tension and give an impression of approachability.

*Un* is commonly used in TJ, or T-Shirt Japanese, to affirm or agree with what the other person says. Textbooks will tell you that the Necktie counterpart of *un* is *hai*, but, in fact, *hai* can sound rather stiff and often smacks of "textbook Japanese." In keeping with the context, one is advised to blend smooth *ee* with the crisper, "aye-aye, sir" sense evoked by *hai*.

コーヒーでもいかがですか？(NJ/MF)
*Kōhii de mo ikaga desu ka?*
Would you like a cup of coffee?
ええ、いただきます。(NJ/MF)

*Ee, itadakimasu.*
Yes, that would be nice.

来月アメリカへいらっしゃるんですってね。(NJ/MF)
*Raigetsu Amerika e irassharu n' desu tte ne.*
So, I hear you're going to America next month.
ええ、そうなんです。(NJ/MF)
*Ee, sō nan desu.*
Yes, we are.

## • *Sō desu* confirms facts or opinions

*Sō desu* is a polite way to agree with a fact or opinion someone
else offers. The T-Shirt equivalent is *sō*.

*Sō desu* "That's right" by itself can sound unpleasantly sharp
and even didactic. Be careful of the situations in which you use it:
it is only appropriate for answering simple questions, or for times
when you want to assert a strong opinion.

コーヒーは110円ですね。(NJ/MF)
*Kōhii wa hyakujū-en desu ne.*
The coffee is 110 yen, right?

(If you are sure that it is, you can say)
　　　そうです。(NJ/MF)
　　　*Sō desu.*
　　　Yup, that's right.

(If you are not sure, or were not previously aware of the 110-
yen price, you can say)
　　　ああ、そうですか。(NJ/MF)
　　　*Ā, sō desu ka.*
　　　Oh, is it?

大江健三郎は、戦後の日本文学でやはり重要な作家でしょう。
　　(NJ/MF)
*Ōe Kenzaburō wa, sengo no Nihon bungaku de yahari jūyō na
　sakka deshō.*
In terms of postwar Japanese literature, Oe Kenzaburo cer-
　tainly comes to mind as an important novelist.

(If you are an authority in the field and agree, or if you agree
without necessarily having a solid basis for doing so, you can say)

そうです。(NJ/MF)
*Sō desu.*
Oh, definitely ("Yes, he is," "I agree").

(If you didn't know that he was important, do not agree, or do not care, you can say)

ああ、そうですか。(NJ/MF)
*Ā, sō desu ka.*
Oh, really?

## • *Arigatō* in Necktie Japanese

*Arigatō* is an important, high-frequency word in both T-Shirt and Necktie Japanese. However, the differences in the word's casual and formal usage are worth remembering. In T-Shirt situations, *arigatō* is used to express gratitude for any kindness, regardless of when it occurred. In NJ, the word can be followed, for extra politeness, by the humble *gozaimasu* or *gozaimashita*, with present or past tense specified.

A good standard for determining whether to use past or present tense when thanking people is to decide whether the kindness is "over" and in the past, or whether it is still having an effect. If it is clearly over, then you should use the past tense. For example, *senjitsu wa gochisō-sama deshita. Arigatō gozaimashita.* "That was a lovely meal (dinner, etc.) the other day (evening). Thank you."

If there is any doubt, you are free to choose either present or past tense, and thus emphasize how grateful you were then, or how much you continue to benefit now. There is no hard-and-fast rule: one store clerk may say *arigatō gozaimasu* when handing customers their change, and another, *arigatō gozaimashita*.

For added emphasis, *dōmo* is often attached before *arigatō* in both T-Shirt and Necktie (see also the section on *dōmo* in Chapter 3, "Tied Up in a Meeting," page 53).

In order to convey the sincerity of your gratitude, it's best to make sure your *arigatō* is clearly enunciated.

# EQUIVALENCY CHART

| T-SHIRT JAPANESE | NECKTIE JAPANESE |
| --- | --- |
| *Anō,* | *Sumimasen,* |
| *kikitai n' da kedo.* | *otazune shitai n' desu ga …* |
| *~ no kashira.* | *~ n' deshō ka.* |
| *~ ?* | *~ desu ka.* |
| *~ yo.* (F) | *~ desu ne.* |
| — | *Sumimasen,* |
| *~ .* | *~ desu.* |
| *~ ne.* | *~ desu ne.* |
| *Un, sō.* | *Ee, sō desu.* |
| *~ yo.* (F) | *~ desu.* |
| *Arigatō.* | *Dōmo arigatō gozaimashita.* |

# At the Airport

## 空港にて

### T-SHIRT JAPANESE

Helen Gally has been visiting Tokyo and is leaving today for home. Her old friend, Yoshiko Yamamura, with whom she has spent a good deal of time with during her stay, goes with her to see her off at the airport.

**Helen:** Thanks a lot for coming to see me off.

**Yoshiko:** No problem. I'm happy to do it.

**Helen:** That was a fantastic meal the other day! Thanks again for everything. I had a great time. Say goodbye to your husband for me.

**Yoshiko:** Thanks. I sure will.

**Helen:** And be sure to come to Los Angeles again to see us.

**Yoshiko:** Oh, thanks! That would be great!

**Helen:** Well, I guess I'd better be going. Take care!

**Yoshiko:** Have a good trip! Bye!

## Tシャツ

ヘレン　わざわざ**見送り**に来てくれてありがとう。

好子　　ううん、とんでもないわ。

ヘレン　**この間**はすっかりごちそうになっちゃって……。いろいろありがとう。**おかげで**すごく楽しかったわ。**ご主人**にもよろしく**伝えて**ね。

好子　ありがとう。そう伝えるわ。

ヘレン　またロサンゼルスにも遊びに来て。

好子　うん、ありがとう。ぜひ。

ヘレン　じゃあこれで。元気でね。

好子　くれぐれも気をつけてね。バイバイ。

## T-SHATSU

**Heren:** *Wazawaza **miokuri ni kite kurete arigatō**.*

**Yoshiko:** *Uun, tonde mo nai wa.*

**Heren:** *Kono aida wa sukkari gochisō ni natchatte … Iroiro arigatō. Okage de sugoku tanoshikatta wa. Goshujin ni mo yoroshiku tsutaete ne.*

**Yoshiko:** *Arigatō. Sō tsutaeru wa.*

**Heren:** *Mata Rosanzerusu ni mo asobi ni kite.*

**Yoshiko:** *Un, arigatō. Zehi.*

**Heren:** *Jā kore de. Genki de ne.*

**Yoshiko:** *Kuregure mo ki o tsukete ne. Baibai.*

### T-SHIRT NOTES

• *Kureru*

*Kureru* is one of several verbs used in Japanese to express the notion of "giving" from the point of view of the recipient. The speaker may be either the recipient or a member of the recipient's in-group.

*Kureru* has a functional role similar to that of the English word "me": it identifies the recipient (which is important in a language which uses its personal pronouns quite sparingly). It also implies that the speaker is the social equal or better of the agent; you wouldn't use *kureru* in reference to something your boss or teacher gave you. It implies gratitude but only moderate deference toward the giver.

In its Necktie form, *kureru* becomes *kudasaru* or *-te (-de) kudasaru*. *Kudasaru* shows a greater level of respect for the person performing the action described. Use *kudasaru* when speaking about the actions of people who are ranked higher on the social scale than you.

| kureru | kudasaru |
|---|---|
| それ、どうしたの? (TJ/MF) | たまにはお手紙くださいね。 |
| *Sore, dō shita no?* | (NJ/MF) |
| Where'd that come from? | *Tama ni wa otegami kudasai ne.* |
| 友達が**くれた**の。(TJ/F) | Write me a letter once in a while. |
| *Tomodachi ga kureta no.* | |
| A friend gave it to me. | |

*Kureru* can be used to mean not only "give me" but also "do for me." It can follow other verbs in their *-te* forms, in order to express the idea that the actor performed the act for the speaker (or for the speaker's in-group) and that the speaker is grateful. Examples of this usage include *kaite kureru* ([be kind enough to] write), *totte kureru* ([kindly] take) and *yonde kureru* ([be so kind as to] read).

For the sake of comparison we could look at the same basic sentence with and without *kureru*. (This sentence could also be formed with *kudasaru* in NJ.)

エリザベスはまたビールを買いに行ったよ。(TJ/M)
*Erizabesu wa mata biiru o kai ni itta yo.*
Elizabeth went to get some beer again.

エリザベスはまたビールを買いに行って**くれた**よ。(TJ/M)
*Erizabesu wa mata biiru o kai ni itte kureta yo.*
Elizabeth went to get us some beer again.

The first sentence above just states the facts, while the second contains a nuance of gratitude. Another example of this distinction might be:

チャールズはさっきトイレに行ったよ。(TJ/M)
*Chāruzu wa sakki toire ni itta yo.*
Charles took himself off to the toilet a minute ago.

チャールズはさっきうちのチビをトイレに連れて行って**くれ**
たよ。(TJ/M)

*Chāruzu wa sakki uchi no chibi o toire ni, tsurete itte **kureta** yo.*

Charles took Junior off to the toilet a minute ago.

Again, in this pattern as well, *kudasaru* can be substituted when the person doing the kind act is one's social better.

| ~ kureru | ~ kudasaru |
|---|---|
| 悪いけど、その塩<br>とって**くれない?** (TJ/MF) | 親切にして**くださって**ありが<br>とうございました。(NJ/MF) |
| *Warui kedo, sono shio*<br>  *totte **kurenai?*** | *Shinsetsu ni shite **kudasatte***<br>  *arigatō gozaimashita.* |
| Sorry, could you pass me<br>  that salt? | Thank you for all your<br>  kindness. |

(For a discussion of the verb *morau*, which is similar to *kureru*, see Chapter Three, "Tied Up In a Meeting," page 51.)

### • *Un* and *uun* for yes and no

*Un*—which one writer has described as a "sublinguistic grunt"— is a T-Shirt version of *hai* ("yes"). Its meaning is often reinforced with a nod of the head. *Uun* is the TJ "no." U-u-N's intonation is distinctive: the voice drops in pitch on the middle vowel, then moves back up, partway, on the final "n."

### • *Tonde mo nai*

*Tonde mo nai* is often used to exclaim that a suggestion is "unthinkable" or "ridiculous." In the dialogue, it is used as a polite way of deflecting someone's thanks.

Unlike *dō itashimashite* "you're welcome," which more or less acknowledges that one has helped the other in some way, *tonde mo nai* suggests that the mere mention of gratitude is quite unnecessary. Necktie equivalents are *tonde mo arimasen* and *tonde mo gozaimasen.*

先日は遅くまでおじゃましてすみませんでした。(NJ/MF)

*Senjitsu wa osoku made ojama shite sumimasen deshita.*

Excuse me for staying so late (at your place) the other day.

いいえ、**とんでもありません**。こちらこそお引きとめして申し訳ありませんでした。(NJ/MF)

*Iie,* **tonde mo arimasen**. *Kochira koso ohikitome shite mōshiwake arimasen deshita.*

Oh, don't be silly. I shouldn't have kept you so long.

### • Expressing gratitude twice

When one has received a gift or a favor or been wined and dined, it is appropriate, of course, to express one's thanks on the spot. In Japan, however, it is also customary to repeat the same formula the next time one speaks to the gift-giver or host of the party, whether in person, in writing or on the telephone. The choice of the simple *kono aida wa dōmo* or the more formal *senjitsu wa dōmo arigatō gozaimashita* ("Thank for your recent kindness") will depend on the nature of the relationship, but in any case the use and, just as importantly, the reuse of these expressions will convey the positive impression of someone who is properly appreciative and who values the relationship.

### • *Gochisō* as a key word for dining

*Gochisō suru* means "to wine and dine (someone)." The kanji *chisō* (馳走) used to write this Sino-Japanese compound suggest preparing the food and drink oneself before settling in to act as host, but *gochisō suru* also functions as a polite equivalent of the native Japanese *ogoru* "treat." When speaking, from the point of the view of the recipient, about being treated to a meal, the phrase is *gochisō ni naru.*

*Gochisō-sama* is a fixed polite phrase spoken before leaving the table at the end of any meal. In the same way, one says *itadakimasu* (lit., "I humbly receive") before beginning to eat, to express generalized gratitude for having the food to eat.

When a guest says *gochisō-sama deshita* after eating your home-cooked meal, the proper response is *osomatsu-sama deshita* "I wish I could have made something much nicer" (lit., "It was rough and crude").

The honorific prefix *go-* is never dropped from the phrase. In T-Shirt and Necktie Japanese alike the word is *gochisō*. Politeness can be increased incrementally by adding *-san, -sama* or *-sama deshita.*

このあいだ**ごちそう**になったシチュー、本当においしかった
わ。(TJ/F)

*Kono aida **gochisō** ni natta shichū, hontō ni oishikatta wa.*

That stew the other day was really great. Thanks!

きょうは私に**ごちそう**させてください。(NJ/MF)

*Kyō wa watashi ni **gochisō** sasete kudasai.*

Let me take you out for lunch (dinner) today./Let me take care
of the check today.

## • -Chatte—the informal contraction of -te shimatte

*Shimau* is a verb that suggests finality of various sorts. It can
mean "to finish doing (do straight through to the end)" or "to
wind up doing." It can also express apprehension or regret about
the action described, or the idea that events have contradicted
your wishes or expectations.

In colloquial speech, the main verb and *shimau* can be joined
to form one word. This is done by conjugating the main verb in its
-*te* form (*wakatte, kaite*), dropping the -*te* and substituting for it -
*chau*, an abbreviated form of *shimau*. Thus we have *wakatchau*
and *kaichau* (or, in the -*te* form, *wakatchatte* and *kaichatte*).
Verbs such as *yomu* which are conjugated into -*de* forms (*yonde*,
etc.) take -*jau* instead of -*chau*.

Finally, when this form is made more casual still, the -*te wa*
can become *chā* or *cha*. Or in the case of the -*de* verbs, -*de wa* can
become *jā* or *ja*.

ひとの日記を読ん**じゃう**なんてひどいわ。(TJ/F)

*Hito no nikki o yon**jau** nan te hidoi wa.*

You've got some nerve, reading my diary.

These contractions are quite common, but nevertheless should
be avoided in very formal situations.

## • Okage de: an expression of gratitude

The fixed phrases *okage de* and *okage-sama de* express gratitude
for blessings received or acts of human kindness. *Okage-sama de*
can express gratitude toward the "powers that be" or, more specifically, toward your listener(s).

Whenever -*sama* is dropped, the gratitude is specific. In the dialogue, Helen's *okage de* is clearly intended to serve as a thank-you to Yoshiko, the listener. With this shorter phrase, it is also possible to specify a third person, distinct from the listener (as in *Fureddo no okage de* "Thanks to Fred").

*Okage-sama de* is often used as a softener in daily conversation. This longer phrase never takes a specifying personal pronoun, and so context alone tells whether the speaker is grateful to "the gods" or to the listener.

Either form eloquently conveys your sense of dependence on good fortune and the goodwill of others.

あなたに教えてもらった**おかげで**迷わずに行けたわ。(TJ/F)
*Anata ni oshiete moratta **okage de** mayowazu ni iketa wa.*
Thanks to the directions you gave me, I was able to find my way there just fine.

君の**おかげで**助かったよ。(TJ/M)
*Kimi no **okage de** tasukatta yo.*
Hey, thanks, I don't know what I would have done without you.

おかあさまはいかがですか？(NJ/MF)
*Okā-sama wa ikaga desu ka?*
How is your mother doing?
**おかげさまで**とても元気になりました。(NJ/F)
***Okage-sama de** totemo genki ni narimashita.*
She's much better, thank you.

息子さん、大学に合格されたんですってね。(NJ/MF)
*Musuko-san, daigaku ni gōkaku sareta n' desu tte ne.*
I hear your son was accepted into university!
ええ、**おかげさまで**。(NJ/MF)
*Ee, **okage-sama de**.*
Yes, we're all very happy about it.

When a speaker wants not to express gratitude but to assign blame for an unfortunate situation, he or she can use a different construction: *(no) sei de* "through the fault of."

きのう飲み過ぎた**せいで**、胃がムカムカするんだ。(TJ/M)
*Kinō nomisugita **sei de**, i ga muka muka suru n' da.*
I drank too much yesterday and now my stomach feels queasy.

Yet, in this same example, the speaker could just as well use *okage de*, since the latter phrase can also be used to describe simple outcomes or results. In this usage, though, *okage de* is broader than *no sei de*, since *okage de* can relate both positive and negative outcomes:

| | |
|---|---|
| 雨が降った**おかげで**、 | • 東京の水不足はすっかり解消しました。 |
| *Ame ga futta **okage de**,* | (NJ/MF) |
| Because of the rain | *Tōkyō no mizu-busoku wa sukkari kaishō shimashita.* |
| | Tokyo's water shortage problem was completely resolved. |
| | • 洗濯物が全然乾きませんよ。(TJ/MF) |
| | *sentakumono ga zenzen kawakimasen yo.* |
| | the laundry hasn't dried a bit. |

Finally, as with the English "thanks to," it is possible to use *okage de* in an ironic, even bitterly sarcastic way.

重好さんに書いてもらった地図の**おかげで**すっかり道に迷っちゃった。(TJ/MF)

*Shigeyoshi-san ni kaite moratta chizu no **okage de** sukkari michi ni mayotchatta.*

Thanks to the map you drew me, Shigeyoshi, I got completely lost.

### • *Sugoku* TJ: very T-Shirt

*Sugoku* is the adverbial form of the adjective *sugoi*. Originally meaning "uncannily, dreadfully, horribly," it has come to be used as an all-purpose intensifier, much like the English "awfully." Intensified still further the adverb becomes *monosugoku*.

While *sugoi* is an adjective used in both TJ and NJ, the adverb *sugoku* suggests a rather colloquial style and is therefore more common in T-Shirt language. Adverbs which can be used in place of *sugoku* to more conservative, NJ effect include *totemo* "quite," *hontō ni* "really" and *taihen* "seriously."

Emotion-laden intensifiers in many languages inspire slangish innovations, particularly among the young, and Japanese is no exception. The adjective *sugoi*, for instance, has been taken over for use as an adverb by young Japanese, e.g. *sugoi kirei* "reaaal beautiful." The proper form, or course, would be *sugoku*. The word *sugoi* should either be followed by a noun, or stand alone.

きょうの映画、**すごく**よかったね。(TJ/MF)
*Kyō no eiga,* **sugoku** *yokatta ne.*
The movie we saw today was awfully good, wasn't it?

あんまりおいしいもんだから、調子に乗って**すごく**食べちゃった。(TJ/MF)
*Anmari oishii mon da kara, chōshi ni notte* **sugoku** *tabechatta.*
The food was so good that I got carried away and ate an awful lot.

### • *Shujin* for your own husband, *goshujin* for everyone else's

*Shujin*, or "husband" (lit., "main person"), originally designated the head of a household. Nowadays, married women use the term when referring to their husbands in the third person, in place of his given name. When you talk about other women's husbands, simply add the honorific prefix *go-*, for *goshujin*.

Some Japanese women object that *shujin* means "master" and that tolerating its usage contributes to the perpetuation of a male-dominated society. These women may use *tsureai* ("companion," "partner") instead. But they remain a small minority, with most continuing to accept the traditional term.

(For more information on what husbands and wives call each other, see also Chapter 6, "Parents and Children's Fitness Day," page 113.)

### • *Yoroshiku*

This adverb is generally used as a formulaic solicitation of the hearer's kindness and good wishes, notably when strangers are introducing themselves to each other. In business relationships, it is also commonly heard when requests for work or services are being made and acknowledged.

When speaking to the hearer of a third party in TJ, *yoroshiku* is a shortened form of (NJ) *yoroshiku otsutae kudasai* "Please give my regards to …" To this you can add such adverbial elements as "*dōzo*," "*dō ka*" or "*kuregure mo*," the last of which means "repeatedly," "earnestly."

(Said, for instance, just before hanging up in a phone call with a client)

どうぞよろしく。(TJ, NJ/MF)

*Dōzo yoroshiku.*

Well then, thank you (that sounds very good, etc.).

(Asking someone older or more prominent than yourself to give your regards to others)

皆様にもどうか**よろしく**お伝えください。(NJ/MF)

*Mina-sama ni mo dō ka **yoroshiku** otsutae kudasai.*

Please do give everyone my regards.

(What your boss might say, for instance, just before going away on a trip and leaving the office in your charge)

くれぐれも**よろしく**頼むよ。(TJ/M)

*Kuregure mo **yoroshiku** tanomu yo.*

I'll leave you to handle things around here, then.

## • *Jā, de wa, sore de wa*

The conjunction *sore de wa* signals a transition between what one has been discussing and the next order of business, including that of taking one's leave. A shortened form is *de wa*, which can also undergo further contraction to *jā*, a phenomenon mentioned earlier. As you might expect, *sore de wa* is more formal than *de wa*, and *de wa* is more formal than *jā*.

じゃあ、さっそく始めよう。(TJ/M)

*Jā, sassoku hajimeyō.*

Well, should we get started?

では、きょうはこのへんで。(TJ, NJ/MF)

*De wa, kyō wa kono hen de.*

Well, then. Let's leave it at this for today.

それでは、またお目にかかりましょう。(NJ/MF)

*Sore de wa, mata ome ni kakarimashō.*

Well, then, see you again.

## • Marking time with *kore*

*Kore* is a demonstrative prounoun which, as you know, usually means "this" and is used to refer to objects which are close at hand for the speaker. However, it can also be used in a temporal sense; in this usage its meaning is "now" or "a point in the very recent past or near future." When used as a marker of time, *kore* is usually followed by a particle such as *kara* ("from"), *yori* ("from") or *made* ("through").

これからそっちへ行ってもいいかしら。(TJ/F)
*Kore kara sotchi e itte mo ii kashira.*
Do you suppose it would be all right for me to drop in on you now?

これまでの経過をご説明申しあげます。(NJ/MF)
*Kore made no keika o gosetsumei mōshiagemasu.*
Let me explain the process through this point.

### • *Baibai*

*Baibai* is, obviously, a borrowing from the English. In American English, this word is sometimes associated with young children, but in Japanese many young people, and especially young women, use it regularly.

*Baibai* is rarely used among people who are middle-aged or older. *Sayōnara* is commonly used among women as they work for the day, although it tends to have a "personal" rather than a professional ring to it. In other situations, you are likely to hear a range of phrases like *sore jā* or *jā, mata kondo*. (See also Chapter 7, "Lovely/Birdbrained Wife," pp. 126 and 131, for other TJ and NJ ways to say good-bye.)

# NECKTIE JAPANESE

Helen Gally has been visiting Tokyo and is leaving today for home. Mrs. Yoshiko Yamamura, a Japanese acquaintance who has been very helpful to Helen during this stay, goes with her to see her off at the airport.

**Gally:** Thank you so much for seeing me off like this!

**Yamamura:** Not at all. It's my pleasure.

**Gally:** That was a wonderful meal the other day. Thank you very much for everything. I had a marvelous time. Give my regards to your husband again.

**Yamamura:** Thank you. I certainly will.

**Gally:** I do hope you will come to Los Angeles again to see us.

**Yamamura:** Oh, thank you. You never know—we just may!

**Gally:** Well, I suppose I should be on my way. Take care of yourself!

**Yamamura:** Have a good trip! Good-bye!


## ネクタイ

ガリー　わざわざお見送りに来てくださってありがとうございました。

山村　いいえ、とんでもございません。

ガリー　**先日**はすっかりごちそうになってしまいまして……。いろいろありがとうございました。**おかげさま**で本当に楽しかったです。どうぞご主人様にもよろしくお伝えくださいませ。

山村　ありがとうございます。そのように申し伝えます。

ガリー　またロサンゼルスの方にもお遊びにいらしてください。

山村　ええ、ありがとうございます。ぜひそうさせていただきます。

ガリー　それではこれで失礼いたします。どうぞお元気で。

山村　くれぐれもお気をつけて。ごめんくださいませ。

## NEKUTAI

**Garii:** *Wazawaza **omiokuri ni kite kudasatte** arigatō gozaimashita.*

**Yamamura:** *Iie, tonde mo gozaimasen.*

**Garii:** *Senjitsu wa sukkari gochisō ni **natte shimaimashite** ... Iroiro **arigatō gozaimashita**. Okagesama de hontō ni tanoshikatta desu. Dōzo goshujin-sama ni mo yoroshiku **otsutae kudasaimase.***

**Yamamura:** *Arigatō gozaimasu. Sono yō ni mōshitsutaemasu.*

**Garii:** *Mata Rosanzerusu **no hō ni mo oasobi ni** irashite kudasai.*

**Yamamura:** *Ee, arigatō gozaimasu. Zehi sō sasete itadakimasu.*

**Garii:** *Sore de wa kore de shitsurei itashimasu. Dōzo ogenki de.*

**Yamamura:** *Kuregure mo **oki o tsukete**. Gomen kudasaimase.*

---

| **NECKTIE NOTES** |

## • Adding prefixes *o-* or *go-* for a Necktie effect

*O-*and *go-*are prefixes that can be attached to nouns to show respect or humility, or to express politeness or to sound refined and elegant.

(1) You can use *o-* and *go-*as honorific markers, by attaching them to objects owned by, or actions performed by, people of a higher social standing, and for whom you want to express respect.

(2) On the other hand, they can also be humble, when attached to nouns that describe actions of yours that affect the listener or someone else.

(3) *O-* and *go-* can also be attached to a wide range of nouns, to create a sense of refinement or elegance. In some words, the *o-* or *go-* has become a more or less undetachable element, as in *ocha* "green tea," *gohan* "cooked rice." This optional use of the prefixes is more common in women's speech.

(1) (To the manager of your department.)
部長、先程ご自宅からお電話がありました。(NJ/MF)
*Bucho, sakihodo **go**jitaku kara **o**denwa ga arimashita.*
You had a telephone call earlier from your wife [or other family member; lit., "from your own home"].

ちょっとお時間をいただけますか。(NJ/MF)
*Chotto **o**jikan o itadakemasu ka.*
Could you give me some time?

(2) ご迷惑をおかけしまして申し訳ありません。(NJ/MF)
***Go**meiwaku o okake shimashite mōshiwake arimasen.*
Please excuse me for causing you so much trouble.

いつお返事をさしあげればよろしいでしょうか。(NJ/MF)
*Itsu **o**henji o sashiagereba yoroshii deshō ka.*
When would you like a reply?

(3) すみませんが、お水いただけませんか。(NJ/MF)
*Sumimasen ga, **o**mizu itadakemasen ka.*
Could I have a glass of water?

ご飯になさいますか。それともパンになさいますか。(NJ/MF)
***Go**han ni nasaimasu ka. Sore tomo pan ni nasaimasu ka.*
Would you like rice or bread (with your meal)?

The kanji 御 is usually pronounced *o-* when attached to words of native Japanese origin, and *go-* when affixed to Sino-Japanese terms. However, not all usages follow this rule and so it is best to memorize the pronunciations that are used with specific words.

As a general rule, *o-* cannot be attached to loanwords from any languages other than Chinese.

### ● The greater formality of Sino-Japanese

One characteristic of Necktie speech is the deliberate greater use of kanji compounds. Words of this type were, as you probably already know, formed by imitating the pronunciation and/or the kanji combinations of Chinese terms. For instance, the phrase *kono aida* "the other day" becomes *senjitsu* in the more formal, Chinese-based equivalent. *Kyō* becomes *honjitsu* and *ashita* becomes *myōnichi*.

### ● *Go- ~ -sama* is very polite

Terms of address used to refer to family members can be made progressively more polite with the addition of prefixes and suffixes. For instance, the plain *shujin* used to refer to one's own husband becomes *goshujin* when you are talking about someone else's husband. For extra politeness, this can also become *goshujin-sama*

In the same way, *ryōshin* ("my parents") becomes *goryōshin* or *goryōshin-sama* (both meaning "your/his/her/their parents").

### ● *-Te kudasai* and *o ~ kudasai*

*Kudasai* is the command form of the verb *kudasaru*. *Kudasai* is used in constructions such as *~ o kudasai* to ask someone to give you a particular object. It is also used, in the construction *-te (-de) kudasai*, to request that someone perform a certain action; in this usage, *kudasai* follows a verb in its *-te (-de)* form, and this verb expresses the action being requested. Both *o- kudasai* and *-te (-de) kudasai* are polite forms used to request action, but *o- kudasai* is more polite, because the honorific prefix *o- (go-)* is attached to the stem of the verb which expresses the action you are asking the other to take; in the case of Sino-Japanese verbs, *go-* replaces *o-*.

3,000 円の回数券をください。(NJ/MF)
*Sanzen-en no kaisū-ken o **kudasai**.*

Give me three thousand yen's worth of commuter tickets, please.

(All NJ/MF)

ここに名前を書いてください。
*Koko ni namae o kaite kudasai.*
こちらにお名前をお書きください。
*Kochira ni onamae o okaki
    kudasai.*
こちらにお名前をご記入ください。
*Kochira ni onamae o gokinyū
    kudasai.*

これを読んでください。
*Kore o yonde kudasai.*
こちらをお読みください。
*Kochira o oyomi kudasai.*

こちらをご一読ください。
*Kochira o goichidoku
    kudasai.*

## • *-Mase* adds a sense of respect

*-Mase* is the command form of *-masu*. It is attached to such verbs as *irassharu* (*irasshaimase*) "come," *kudasaru* (*kudasaimase*) "give" and *nasaru* (*nasaimase*) "do" for its softening effect. The pattern was originally characteristic of women's speech but then came to be used by merchants as well, for the respectful tone it suggested. The most common usage nowadays is the *irasshaimase* "Welcome!" heard with particular frequency in shops and boutiques where the greater number of customers are women.

## • *Mōshitsutaemasu*

*Mōshitsutaemasu* is a humbler way of saying *tsutaeru* or "I'll pass along the message." It is commonly used in cases in which the message to be relayed is intended for a member of one's own in-group, especially a member of one's own family or a colleague at work.

## • *Irashite* particularly common in women's speech

*Irashite* is an alternative form of *irasshatte*. Perhaps because its sound is thought to be softer, it is particularly common in women's speech. Both *irashite* and *irasshatte* serve as the honorific forms of the verbs *iru* ("to be"), *iku* ("to go") and *kuru* ("to come").

佐藤さんなら、先程までここにいらしたのに残念ですね。
    (NJ/MF)

*Sato-san nara, sakihodo made koko ni **irashita** no ni zannen
    desu ne.*

Ms. Satō? She was here until just a while ago, but I'm afraid
    you've missed her.

コンサートのチケットが 2 枚あるんですが、よかったらいら
っしゃいませんか。(NJ/MF)

*Konsāto no chiketto ga nimai aru n' desu ga, yokattara
    **irasshai**masen ka.*

I happen to have two tickets to the concert. Would you be
    interested in going?

● *-Sete itadaku*

*-Sete itadaku* is a humble way to let the listener know that you
would like to do something. Literally, it would mean something
like "I presume to be allowed to …" It is even more humble than
its variant *-sete morau.*

Depending on the verb used, the form sometimes becomes
*-sasete itadaku.*

ぜひうかがわせていただきます。(NJ/MF)

*Zehi ukagawa**sete itadakimasu.***

I will be very happy to call on you.

(In a store)

このスーツを試着させていただきたいんですが。(NJ/MF)

*Kono sūtsu o shichaku **sasete itadakitai** n' desu ga.*

I would like to try on this suit.

この件については、考えさせていただきます。(NJ/MF)

*Kono ken ni tsuite wa, kangae**sasete itadakimasu.***

I will have to think the matter over a little more.

では、来週もう一度お電話させていただきます。(NJ/MF)

*De wa, raishū mō ichido odenwa **sasete itadakimasu.***

So then, I will phone you again next week.

● *Sayōnara* **not often used in Necktie Japanese**

There are many ways to say good-bye, but in NJ the most common are *shitsurei shimasu, shitsurei itashimasu, shitsurei sasete
itadakimasu,* and *gomen kudasai.* Of these, *shitsurei shimasu* is

perhaps the most widely used. The more polite variant is *shitsurei itashimasu*.

*Shitsurei shimasu*, the most common form, has a kind of a light touch. Since *shitsurei itashimasu* uses the humbler form *itasu* in place of *suru*, it is more polite. The still more polite *shitsurei sasete itadakimasu* can be used, for instance, if you a leave a party early, and thus are actually apologizing for leaving ahead of the others. *Gomen kudasai* is, of course, a set expression used for entering someone else's home; it can also be used when you leave.

● *Kuregure mo*

*Kuregure mo* literally means "repeatedly." It reinforces the intensity or sincerity of your request. The phrase is often used during the course of saying good-bye.

くれぐれもよろしくお願い申し上げます。(NJ/MF)
*Kuregure mo yoroshiku onegai mōshiagemasu.*
Please give my best regards to ...

くれぐれもお大事になさってください。(NJ/MF)
*Kuregure mo odaiji ni nasatte kudasai.*
Do take care of yourself!

● *Oki o tsukete*: a cautionary *bon voyage*

In English, one typically emphasizes the positive when bidding farewell to friends and acquaintances who are going off on a journey: "Have a good trip" or "Enjoy your trip." In Japanese, on the other hand, the farewells are a shade more cautionary, as in, for instance, *oki o tsukete* "Look after yourself"; *dōzo gobuji de* "Come back safe and sound."

## EQUIVALENCY CHART

| T-SHIRT JAPANESE | NECKTIE JAPANESE |
| --- | --- |
| miokuri ni | omiokuri ni |
| kite kurete | kite kudasatte |
| arigatō. | arigatō gozaimashita. |

| | |
|---|---|
| *Uun,* | *Iie,* |
| *tonde mo nai wa.* | *tonde mo gozaimasen.* |
| *Kono aida wa* | *Senjitsu wa* |
| *natchatte ...* | *natte shimaimashite* |
| *arigatō.* | *arigatō gozaimashita.* |
| *Okage de* | *Okage-sama de* |
| *sugoku* | *hontō ni* |
| *~ wa.* (F) | *~ desu.* |
| — | *Dōzo* |
| *Goshujin* | *goshujin-sama* |
| *tsutaete ne.* | *otsutae kudaisaimase.* |
| *Arigatō.* | *Arigatō gozaimasu.* |
| *Sō* | *Sono yō ni* |
| *tsutaeru wa.* | *mōshitsutaemasu.* |
| *~ ni mo* | *~ no hō ni mo* |
| *asobi ni* | *oasobi ni* |
| *kite.* | *irashite kudasai.* |
| *Un,* | *Ee,* |
| *Arigatō.* | *arigatō gozaimasu.* |
| *Zehi.* | *Zehi sō sasete itadakimasu.* |
| *Jā* | *Sore de wa* |
| *kore de.* | *kore de shitsurei itashimasu.* |
| *Genki de ne.* | *Dōzo ogenki de.* |
| *ki o tsukete ne.* | *oki o tsukete.* |
| *Baibai.* | *Gomen kudasaimase.* |

# Tied Up in a Meeting

## ただいま会議中

### T-SHIRT JAPANESE

Sandra Lang is the manager of the Yamato Soccer Club. Shin Yasuda, a trainer at the fitness club which Sandra and team member Mr. Nozaki frequent, calls and asks for Mr. Nozaki. Unfortunately, Mr. Nozaki is in a meeting.

**Sandra:** Yamato Soccer Club.
**Shin:** Hello. This is Yasuda of the Athletes Sports Club.
**Sandra:** Oh, hello!
**Shin:** Hi, Sandra. Is Nozaki there?
**Sandra:** Oh, sorry. He's in a meeting right now.
**Shin:** Okay. Could you ask him to call me?
**Sandra:** Sure, I'll let him know.
**Shin:** Thanks!
**Sandra:** Thanks for calling. Bye.

### Tシャツ

サンドラ　やまとサッカークラブです。
慎　　　　もしもし、アスリーツの安田だけど。
サンドラ　こんにちは。
慎　　　　こんにちは。あのう、野崎さんいる？
サンドラ　ごめんね。いまミーティング中なの。

| 慎 | あ、そう。それじゃあ、安田まで電話もらいたいんだけど。 |
| サンドラ | うん、わかった。そう伝えるわ。 |
| 慎 | よろしく。 |
| サンドラ | どうも。 |

# T-SHATSU

| Sandora: | *Yamato Sakkā Kurabu* **desu.** |
| Shin: | *Moshimoshi, Asuriitsu no Yasuda* **da kedo.** |
| Sandora: | **Konnichiwa.** |
| Shin: | **Konnichiwa.** *Anō, Nozaki-san* **iru?** |
| Sandora: | **Gomen ne. Ima miitingu-***chū* **na no.** |
| Shin: | *A, sō. Sore jā, Yasuda made* **denwa moraitai n' da kedo.** |
| Sandora: | **Un, wakatta. Sō tsutaeru wa.** |
| Shin: | **Yoroshiku.** |
| Sandora: | **Dōmo.** |

---

### T-SHIRT NOTES

---

• *Moshimoshi* **when making a telephone call**

*Moshimoshi* is the form of "hello" used on the telephone. Originally it served as a way to get the attention of passersby and others whose names were unknown. It is still used in that way, but now is much more specifically associated with the telephone.

• **The importance of giving your group's name first, then your own**

In the dialogue, Mr. Yasuda identifies himself not only with his own name but with that of his employer first, in the pattern "*(company) no ~ desu,*" as is customary in business calls to clients.

When you phone or stop in somewhere and ask for a specific individual, you should not only give your own name but also place yourself in context, mentioning the name of your company, your school, some leisure-time interest that you share with the person you want to speak with, or some other connection between you.

## • Dropping the *wa* when you ask for someone on the phone

Strictly speaking, the way to ask for someone on the phone is *Nozaki-san wa irasshaimasu ka*. But in fact people quite commonly leave off the topic particle *wa*. It's considered easier and smoother to say *Nozaki-san irasshaimasu ka*. In the same way, you can also omit the object particle *o*, which is—properly speaking—used with transitive verbs. Both of these contractions occur more often in T-Shirt speech than in Necktie.

> (omitting *wa*)
> 菅原さん(は)もう帰った? (TJ/MF)
> *Sugawara-san (wa) mō kaetta?*
> Has Sugawara-san left (for the day) already?

> (omitting *o*)
> 伊藤さん(を)知ってる? (TJ/MF)
> *Itō-san (o) shitte 'ru?*
> You know Itō-san?

## • *Gomen* as an expression of apology in TJ

In T-Shirt Japanese, *gomen nasai* can be abbreviated as *gomen*, often followed by a particle. Thus, *gomen yo* for men, and *gomen ne* for men and women.

> あ、ごめん、痛かった? (TJ/MF)
> *A, gomen, itakatta?*
> Oh, sorry! That hurt?

> さっきはごめんね。(TJ/MF)
> *Sakki wa gomen ne.*
> Sorry about that just now.

> 遅れてごめんよ。(TJ/M)
> *Okurete gomen yo.*

Sorry to be late.

## • Sorting out the different meanings of *sō*

*Sō* is basically used to affirm or express agreement with what the other is saying. But the various uses of *sō* take some sorting out.

First of all, *a sō?* (TJ) or *a sō desu ka* (NJ) can be used to reply to something you didn't know before ("Oh, really?"). In this case, the *ka* does not indicate any actual doubt, and so the intonation falls on this syllable. That way, the phrase sounds not like a question or a challenge, but like a simple statement.

川村さんに男の子が生まれたんだって。(TJ/MF)
*Kawamura-san ni otoko no ko ga umaretan datte.*
I heard Kawamura-san has had a baby boy.
あ、そう。(TJ/MF)
*A, sō.*
That so?

進藤さん、アメリカに留学されたらしいですよ。(NJ/MF)
*Shindō-san, Amerika ni ryūgaku sareta rashii desu yo.*
It seems Shindō-san has gone to America to study.
あ、そうですか。(NJ/MF)
*A, sō desu ka.*
I see.

If you give your *sō* some emphasis and a somewhat higher inflection throughout, this suggests that you're surprised at the new information.

きのうなくしたお財布、出てきたのよ。(TJ/F)
*Kinō naku shita osaifu, dete kita no yo.*
Hey, you know, that coin purse I lost yesterday turned up!
あ、そう、よかったね。(TJ/MF)
*A, sō, yokatta ne.*
Oh, really? That's good.

昨年体調をこわして入院しまして……。(NJ/MF)
*Sakunen taichō o kowashite nyūin shimashite ...*
I wasn't feeling well last year and ended up in the hospital.
そうですか。それは大変でしたね。(NJ/MF)

*Sō desu ka. Sore wa taihen deshita ne.*
Really! I'm sorry to hear that.

If someone asks you a question about a topic that you are very familiar with, a T-Shirt *un, sō* or the more formal *ee/hai, sō desu* is appropriate.

これ君の? (TJ/M)
*Kore kimi no?*
This yours?
うん、そうよ。(TJ/F)
*Un, sō yo.*
Yeah, it's mine.

これで荷物は全部ですか。(NJ/MF)
*Kore de nimotsu wa zenbu desu ka.*
Is this all your luggage?
はい、そうです。(NJ/MF)
*Hai, sō desu.*
Yes, that's all of it.

If a person gives their thoughts on a subject about which you also have an opinion or strong feelings, and you agree with their assessment, you can say *un, sō da ne* (TJ/M) or *un, sō ne* (TJ/F) or *ee (hai) sō desu ne* (NJ/MF).

きょうは蒸し暑いわね。(TJ/F)
*Kyō wa mushiatsui wa ne.*
It's pretty muggy today, don't you think.
うん、そうだね。(TJ/M)
*Un, sō da ne.*
Sure is.

地震って本当に怖いですね。(NJ/MF)
*Jishin tte hontō ni kowai desu ne.*
It's pretty scary thinking about earthquakes, you know?
ええ、そうですね。(NJ/MF)
*Ee, sō desu ne.*
I know what you mean.

(For a discussion of *tte*, see Chapter 6, "Parent and Children's

Fitness Day," p. 107; for the various uses and meanings of *sō desu*, see Chapter 1, "Where Do I Change Trains," p. 23.)

If you want to disagree or express some doubt, a simple *sō?* or *sō desu ka* will do. However, it's important to note here that the intonation is different than in the other usages of *sō*. Here, the word is long and drawn out, with the inflection first falling, and then rising again: *SO-o-O?* In the case of *sō desu ka*, the inflection rises on the *ka*, showing that it is an actual question.

> あの映画おもしろかったよ。(TJ/M)
> *Ano eiga omoshirokatta yo.*
> That was an interesting movie!
> そう(お)?　私はそうは思わなかったけど。(TJ/F)
> *Sō(o)? watashi wa sō wa omowanakatta kedo.*
> Really? *I* didn't think so.

> 私はA案の方がいいと思います。(NJ/MF)
> *Watashi wa A-an no hō ga ii to omoimasu.*
> I think Plan A is better.
> そうですか。私はB案も悪くないと思いますが……。(NJ/MF)
> *Sō desu ka. Watashi wa B-an mo waruku nai to omoimasu ga.*
> Really? I kind of like Plan B, too.

## • T-Shirt is often shorter than Necktie

TJ verb forms are shorter and simpler than NJ verb forms; so are TJ utterances in general. Necktie speech tends to be longer, more complicated, and full of Sino-Japanese. Comparing the dialogues above, for example, we can see that the *sō* of the TJ phrase *sō tsutaeru wa* is "stretched out" to *sono yō ni* in NJ. Likewise, *kō* becomes *kono yō ni*; *ā*, *ano yō ni*; and *dō* becomes *dono yō ni*.

## • *Morau* and *itadaku*

*Morau* is a verb meaning "to receive." In its simplest sense, it can refer to objects received. In this usage, *morau* is neutral and does not have the same built-in sense of gratitude implied by *kureru* (give me). The more humble NJ equivalent is *itadaku*.

> それ、どうしたの? (TJ/MF)
> *Sore, dō shita no?*

Where did that come from?

友達にもらったの。(TJ/F)

*Tomodachi ni moratta no.*

I got it from a friend.

ラルフ・サムナー先生からクリスマスカードをいただきました。(NJ/MF)

*Rarufu Samunā sensei kara kurisumasu kādo o itadakima-shita.*

I got a Christmas card from my old teacher, Ralph Sumner.

*Morau* can be used in reference to profiting from some action. When used in this way, it follows a verb conjugated in the *-te* (*-de*) form. *-Te morau* does not contain the same nuance of gratitude which *-te kureru* does. The recipient of the action is pleased by the result when either of these verbs is used, but *kureru* more straightforwardly expresses thankfulness.

This same *-te* (*-de*) *morau* form is also used to refer to action that someone requested of someone else: "have somebody do," "get somebody to do." So, for example, *katte morau* ("buy for me [for somebody]"), *shite morau* ("have you [someone] do") or *kaite morau* ("get someone to write").

Please note here an important difference between *kureru* and *morau*. *Kureru* is always used from the standpoint of "me/I/us"; in other words, it means "give me (us/someone close to me)." *Morau*, though, can be used about anybody, to mean "I receive," "he receives," etc. The *-te morau* form, of course, becomes *-de morau* with verbs such as *yomu* (*yonde*), where "*n*" precedes the final syllable.

In the Necktie Japanese of this second usage as well, *morau* becomes *itadaku*, and so *-te morau* becomes *-te itadaku*.

手伝ってもらって本当に助かったよ。(TJ/M)

*Tetsudatte moratte hontō ni tasukatta yo.*

Thank you very much. You were a big help!

もう一度説明していただけませんか。(NJ/MF)

*Mō ichido setsumei shite itadakemasen ka.*

Could you please explain that once more?

(See also the explanation of *kureru*, which is similar to *morau* in both meaning and usage, in Chapter 2, page 27.)

## • The handiness of *dōmo*

*Dōmo* is often used by itself as a brief, casual word appropriate for quick thanks or apologies. It can also be attached to thanks or apologies, to lend them extra emphasis. Originally, *dōmo* was strictly an emphatic modifier, but now is also frequently heard as a T-Shirt contraction which stands on its own, resonating the unspoken longer phrases.

(All NJ/MF)
どうも(ありがとう)。
*Dōmo (arigatō).*
Thank you.

どうも(すみません)。
*Dōmo (sumimasen).*
Pardon me.

どうも(お世話になっております)。
*Dōmo (osewa ni natte orimasu).*
Thank you (for all you have done).

先日はどうも(お疲れさまでした)。
*Senjitsu wa **dōmo** (otsukare-sama deshita).*
I really appreciate your hard work the other day.

その節はどうも(お世話になりました)。
*Sono setsu wa **dōmo** (osewa ni narimashita).*
Thank you very much (that time, you were very kind).

# NECKTIE JAPANESE

Sandra Lang is an intern with the sales department of Sakura Trading Company. A call from a client has just come in for Mr. Nozaki, chief of Sandra's section. Unfortunately, Mr. Nozaki is in a meeting.

**Lang:** Sakura Trading Company, Sales Department.

**Yasuda:** Hello. My name is Shin Yasuda. I'm with the Yamato Leasing Company.

**Lang:** Ah, yes, good afternoon, Mr. Yasuda.

**Yasuda:** Good afternoon to you. Could I speak with Mr. Nozaki, please?

**Lang:** I'm terribly sorry. At the moment he's tied up in a meeting.

**Yasuda:** I see. Well, I'd be grateful if you would ask him to call me.

**Lang:** Very good, sir. Mr. Yasuda of the Yamato Leasing Company. I'll give him the message.

**Yasuda:** Thank you.

**Lang:** Good-bye.

## ネクタイ

ラング　さくら商事営業部でございます。

安田　　もしもし、やまとリースの安田と申しますが……。

ラング　**いつもお世話になっております。**

安田　　**こちらこそお世話様です。**あのう、野崎さんいらっしゃいますか。

ラング　申し訳ございません。ただいま野崎は会議中でございますが……。

安田　あ、そうですか。それでは恐れ入りますが、安田までお電話いただきたいんですが……。

ラング　やまとリースの安田様ですね。かしこまりました。そのように申し伝えます。

安田　よろしくお願いします。

ラング　失礼いたします。


## NEKUTAI

**Lang:** *Sakura Shōji, eigyō-bu de gozaimasu.*

**Yasuda:** *Moshimoshi, Yamato Riisu no Yasuda to mōshimasu ga …*

**Lang:** *Itsumo osewa ni natte orimasu.*

**Yasuda:** *Kochira koso osewa-sama desu. Anō, Nozaki-san irasshaimasu ka.*

**Lang:** *Mōshiwake gozaimasen. Tadaima Nozaki wa kaigi-chū de gozaimasu ga …*

**Yasuda:** *A, sō desu ka. Sore de wa osoreirimasu ga, Yasuda made odenwa itadakitai n' desu ga …*

**Lang:** *Yamato Riisu no Yasuda-sama desu ne. Kashiko-marimashita. Sono yō ni mōshitsutaemasu.*

**Yasuda:** *Yoroshiku onegai shimasu.*

**Lang:** *Shitsurei itashimasu.*


| NECKTIE NOTES |

• **Giving your own name**

Since it's impossible to know who's calling when you pick up a ringing phone, it's best to be politely formal. People generally use either ~ *desu* or ~ *de gozaimasu* as a greeting in this situation.

*De gozaimasu* is equivalent to *desu*, but more polite. It combines the polite verb *gozaru* "be," "exist," with the *-masu* verb ending.

*To mōshimasu* ("My name is") is often used when giving your name to someone you expect has not heard your name before. It combines *mōsu*, the humbler equivalent of the verb *iu* ("to say"), with the *-masu* ending.

### • Set expressions to use on the telephone

Other handy phrases to use in telephone conversations include the following. When you take a call or message for your co-worker, Ms. Smith, you can ask the caller's name by saying *shitsurei desu ga, dochira-sama deshō ka, shitsurei desu ga onamae wa* ... or simply *shitsurei desu ga....*"

When the caller gives his or her name, it is customary for you to say *osewa ni natte orimasu* ("We are/Ms. Smith is indebted to you") or *osewa-sama desu*, even if you have never heard the name before. The word *sewa* when used in this phrase is always preceded by the honorific prefix *o-*, and is usually followed by *-sama* and then by the humble verb *oru* ("be," "exist") in the polite *orimasu* form.

If Ms. Smith is not in the office you should say, *osoreirimasu ga, tadaima gaishutsu shite orimasu ga* "I'm sorry, she is not in the office at the moment." It's important to remember not to attach *-san* to Smith's name since she is part of your in-group. If you expect her back shortly, you can say, *osoreirimasu ga, tadaima seki o hazushite orimasu ga* ... "I'm sorry, but she is away from her desk at the moment." Trailing off with *ga* at the end of your sentence shows that you are waiting politely for some response from the caller.

Finally you can ask whether the caller would like Ms. Smith to telephone back: *modorimashitara odenwa sashiagemasu* or *orikaeshi denwa sasemasu/sashiagemashō ka* ("I will/shall I have her call you").

And of course it is probably best to ask for any caller's telephone number, just in case. You can do this with the phrase *nen no tame odenwa-bangō o onegai (ita)shimasu.*

The set phrase *itsumo X ga osewa ni natte imasu (orimasu)* is used as a kind of greeting when telephone calls come into the home for some other member of the family. In this formula, X can be either the person's first name or their relationship to the speaker, as in *chichi* ("my father"), *haha* ("my mother"), *imōto* ("my younger sister"), *otōto* ("my younger brother"), *musuko* ("my son") and so on. A family member will say this polite formula as soon as the caller gives his or her name on the telephone, provided that the name is somewhat familiar.

### • *Orimasu* as a humble form

*Oru* is a humble equivalent of *iru* ("be," "exist"). *Orimasu* is the more polite form, and often expresses in-group humility toward an out-group.

Like *imasu*, *orimasu* can follow the gerund (*-te*) form of the verb to express ongoing action or conditions.

3時に駅前の喫茶店でお待ちして**おります**。(NJ/MF)
*Sanji ni eki-mae no kissaten de omachi-shite **orimasu**.*
I'll be waiting in the coffee shop in front of the station at three.

おうわさはかねがねうかがって**おります**。(NJ/MF)
*Ouwasa wa kanegane ukagatte **orimasu**.*
I've heard so many good things about you.

### • *Kochira, sochira, achira, dochira*

*Kochira* is, as we saw earlier, a *kosoado* word meaning "this side." It is also used in various polite phrases.

For instance, the *kochira koso* of the dialogue is a polite formula used in response to thanks or apologies. It is an multi-purpose phrase meaning, "Likewise, I'm sure," "The pleasure is all mine" or, as in the dialogue, "No, no, it is us (who are indebted to you)."

*Kochira* and the three other *kosoado* words from this word group are commonly used in two ways:

(1) to specify literal place or direction ("here," "there"); and
(2) to refer to people. In this second usage, *kochira* can take either of two meanings. You can use it to refer to yourself (*kochira wa* "I/we," "as for me/us") or to introduce/refer to a person standing close to you, usually while gesturing toward them (*kochira wa* "this is …").

(1) どうぞこちらへ。(NJ/MF)
*Dōzo kochira e.*
Please come right this way.

そちらの天気はいかがですか。(NJ/MF)
*Sochira no tenki wa ikaga desu ka.*
How is the weather there (where you are)?

(To make polite conversation concerningan unspecified location)
あちらでは何をなさっていたんですか。(NJ/MF)
*Achira de wa nani o nasatte ita n' desu ka.*
What brought you there?

どちらからいらっしゃったんですか。(NJ/MF)
*Dochira kara irasshatta n' desu ka.*
Where are you from?

(2) こちらは東京の鈴木と申しますが、北上さんいらっしゃいますか? (NJ/MF)
*Kochira wa Tōkyō no Suzuki to mōshimasu ga, Kitagami-san irasshaimasu ka?*
This is Suzuki calling from Tokyo. Would Mr. Kitagami be there, please?

こちらは大学時代の恩師の関場先生です。(NJ/MF)
*Kochira wa daigaku jidai no onshi no Sekiba-sensei desu.*
I would like to introduce Professor Sekiba, who was my mentor at university.

そちらの方からお電話いただけますか。(NJ/MF)
*Sochira no hō kara odenwa itadakemasu ka.*
Would it be possible for you to call me?

あちらはどなたですか。(NJ/MF)
*Achira wa donata desu ka.*
Who's that over there?

(Used on the telephone and when the doorbell rings)
どちら様ですか。(NJ/MF)
*Dochira-sama desu ka.*
May I ask who is calling?/Who's there?

● **Asking for someone on the phone**

If you aren't sure whether the person you want to speak with is actually there, you can say, ~ -san irasshaimasu ka or ~ -san irasshaimasu deshō ka. Please note that that this is a set polite phrase which even in this Necktie form does not require the particle "wa."

If you are sure that the person is there, you can just say ~ -san o onegai shitain desu ga....

• *Moshiwake gozaimasen ga*: **Sorry, but**

Mōshiwake gozaimasen is a rather formal way of making an apology. In descending order of politeness, there are also mōshiwake arimasen and mōshiwake nai (this last T-Shirt, but still respectful). Other apologetic expressions include the T-Shirt gomen or sumanai and the more formal gomen nasai or sumimasen. Please note that though gomen nasai is used strictly for apologies, sumimasen can also be used to cut in on a conversation or to get someone's attention.

• **Never use -san for those in your in-group**

When talking about someone who is a member of your own family, company, or organization (your in-group) to an outsider, you never add -san or use any other honorifics. Inside the company, for example, you call your section chief by his title, kachō, as a sign of respect, but if a telephone call comes in for him from a client or someone else on the outside, you would refer to him by his last name without -san.

• *Osoreirimasu*: **Beg your pardon**

The expression osoreirimasu is the basic form of thanks used in many Necktie situations. It is also often used in more casual situations to thank someone who does something for you which was unexpectedly kind and thoughtful. It combines a nuance of thanks with one of apology, and so is quite polite.

(See also the explanation of kyōshuku desu in Chapter 4, page 71.)

• **Avoiding abrupt statements**

A number of sentences in the dialogue end with ga ... as a means of avoiding abruptness. These include, "Yamato Riisu no Yasuda to *mōshimasu ga …*," "*Tadaima Nozaki wa kaigichū de goza-imasu ga …*" and "*Yasuda made odenwa itadakitain desu ga ….*" This kind of statement sounds polite because it takes any rough edges off what you have said by inviting the other person to respond. Related to the desire to give the speaker room to maneuver is a fondness for euphemism and circumlocution, use of which is considered a mark of refinement.

## • In business contexts, always confirm messages

In formal business exchanges, it's considered proper to repeat the content of any message you take, in order to avoid misunderstandings, omissions and errors. In the dialogue, when Sandra Lang says, *Yamato Riisu no Yasuda-san desu ne*, she is doing this kind of careful double-check. And when there is any doubt, for instance, about how to write a name in Chinese characters, the person taking the message may apologetically ask for such details as well.

念のためお電話番号をお願いいたします。(NJ/MF)
*Nen no tame odenwa-bango o onegai itashimasu.*
Let me take your phone number, just to be sure.

*Nen no tame* is a set phrase meaning "just in case." Of course, the honorific *onegai (ita)shimasu* and the *o-* of *odenwa* both let the other person know immediately that it is *their* telephone number you are asking for.

## • *Kashikomarimashita*

This expression is used toward superiors as a humble expression of assent to orders or requests. More casual equivalents would include *un*, *hai* and *wakatta*. *Wakarimashita* is similar but is used mainly toward equals or those ranked lower than you on the social scale, whereas *kashikomarimashita* is used by shop clerks to customers and in other situations where the speaker is clearly required to defer to the listener.

# EQUIVALENCY CHART

| T-SHIRT JAPANESE | NECKTIE JAPANESE |
| --- | --- |
| ~ desu. | ~ de gozaimasu. |
| ~ da kedo. | ~ to mōshimasu ga ... |
| Konnichiwa. | Itsumo osewa ni natte ori-masu. |
| Konnichiwa. | Kochira koso osewa-sama desu. |
| iru? | irasshaimasu ka. |
| Gomen ne. | Mōshiwake gozaimasen. |
| Ima | tadaima |
| — | Nozaki wa |
| miitingu | kaigi |
| ~ na no. (F) | ~ de gozaimasu ga ... |
| sō. | sō desu ka. |
| Sore jā, | Sore de wa |
| — | osoreirimasu ga, |
| denwa moraitai n' da kedo. | odenwa itadakitai n' desu ga ... |
| — | Yamato Riisu no Yasuda-sama desu ne. |
| Un, wakatta. | Kashikomarimashita. |
| Sō | Sono yō ni |
| tsutaeru wa. (F) | mōshitsutaemasu. |
| Yoroshiku. | Yoroshiku onegai shimasu. |
| Dōmo. | Shitsurei itashimasu. |

# Exchanging Business Cards

## 名刺交換

## T-SHIRT JAPANESE

Stefan Poggendorf, who works for Theiss Pharmaceuticals, drops in on former university classmate Masayuki Kubota at Kubota's company. The two men have not seen each other in some years.

**Stefan:** Hi! Thanks a lot for taking the time to see me! (Hands Yoshio his business card) Let me give you my newest business card. Here you go.

**Masayuki:** (Takes the card and gives Stefan his own) Thanks. (Points to a chair) Sit down!

**Stefan:** Thanks.

**Masayuki:** By the way, isn't this the first time you've been to our new office?

**Stefan:** Yep. What a nice place you have here. You even have a great view of Tokyo Bay.

**Masayuki:** Yeah, it's not too bad.


## Tシャツ

シュテファン　やあ。きょうは忙しいのに時間をとってもらってすまないね。(名刺を差し出して)これタイス製薬の新しい名刺、よろしく。

正幸　(名刺を受け取り、自分の名刺を差し出して)よろしく。(椅子を示して)まあすわれよ。

| シュテファン | どうも。 |
| 正幸 | ところで、うちの新しいオフィスに来たのは初めてだったっけ。 |
| シュテファン | うん。なかなかいい所だね。東京湾も見渡せるし。 |
| 正幸 | まあね。 |

## T-SHATSU

**Shutefan:** *Yā. Kyō wa isogashii no ni jikan o totte moratte sumanai ne. (Meishi o sashidashite) Kore Taisu Sei-yaku no atarashii meishi, yoroshiku.*

**Masayuki:** *(Meishi o uketori, jibun no meishi o sashidashite) Yoroshiku. (Isu o shimeshite) Mā suware yo.*

**Shutefan:** *Dōmo.*

**Masayuki:** *Tokoro de, uchi no atarashii ofisu ni kita no wa hajimete dattakke.*

**Shutefan:** *Un. Nakanaka ii tokoro da ne. Tōkyō-wan mo miwataseru shi.*

**Masayuki:** *Mā ne.*

---

| T-SHIRT NOTES |

• *Yā* as a casual male greeting

*Yā* is a casual exclamation used by males:

やあ、しばらく。(TJ/M)
*Yā, shibaraku.*
Hey, it's been a long time!

やあ、元気？(TJ/M)
*Yā, genki?*
Hey there, how's it going?

It is often used as an informal replacement for *ohayō* "Good morning," *konnichiwa* "Good afternoon" or *konbanwa* "Good evening."

*Yō* is similar, but with the difference that, unlike *yā*, it sounds too rough to be used when addressing women. It is generally restricted to close-knit male networks.

## • *Sumanai* the TJ equivalent of *sumimasen*

*Sumanai* is the T-Shirt version of the expression *sumimasen*. It can be used for (1) apologizing, (2) giving thanks and (3) making requests. Compared to *sumimasen*, *sumanai* has a rather rough or perfunctory tone, and is therefore largely restricted to usage by male intimates, or by people in positions of authority when addressing subordinates.

(1) 君には迷惑ばかりかけて**すまない**ね。(TJ/M)
   *Kimi ni wa meiwaku bakari kakete **sumanai** ne.*
   Sorry for all the trouble (I'm causing you).

(2) 俺の車を使えよ。(TJ/M)
   *Ore no kuruma o tsukae yo.*
   Use my car.
   **すまない**な。じゃあ、ちょっと借りるよ。(TJ/M)
   ***Sumanai** na. Jā, chotto kariru yo.*
   Great, thanks. I'll bring it back right away.

(3) **すまない**けど、たばこ買ってきてくれないか。(TJ/M)
   ***Sumanai** kedo, tabako katte kite kurenai ka.*
   Say, could you pick me up a pack of cigarettes?

## • Three different uses of *mā*

*Mā* is used to (1) encourage the listener to perform a certain action, (2) gently put a damper on some impulse of your own or someone else's and (3) express conditional (or stoical) acceptance of a situation which is not quite good enough but which will have to do.

The third meaning is implied particularly when the word is used in the phrase *mā ne* ... This is what we see in the dialogue when the speaker receives a compliment and, rather than openly refute it, deflects it.

(1) まあ一杯いこう。(TJ/M)

*Mā ippai ikō.*
Let's go for a drink, what do you say.
(Or, at the table, glass in hand) Let's drink up!

(2) まああわてないで様子を見ましょう。(TJ/MF)
*Mā awatenai de yōsu o mimashō.*
Now, let's keep our heads and see what happens.

(3) まあいいか。(TJ/M)
*Mā ii ka.*
Yeah, well, that's the way it goes, I guess.

### • *Uchi* designates your "in-group"

*Uchi* is typically used to indicate your own family, house or household—or families in general—but it can also refer to a group or organization (firm, company, office or school) to which one belongs. For example, *uchi no gakkō* "my school," *uchi no kaisha* "our company."

うちの社長、ゴルフが大好きでね。(TJ/MF)
*Uchi no shachō, gorufu ga daisuki de ne.*
The president (of our company) likes golf a lot, you know.

うちでは、そういったものは取り扱っておりませんが……。
(NJ/MF)
*Uchi de wa, sō itta mono wa toriatsukatte orimasen ga …*
We do not carry that kind of item here (in the shop/department store).

### • *-Kke* as a strictly colloquial term

In the classical literary language, *-keri* has the function of making sentences past-tense. *-Keri* is also a retrospective or exclamatory suffix (*kono eda kuno eda chiri ni keri* "The flowers have gone from all the trees"). *-Kke* derives from this form, and is a contracted colloquialism. It can be used (1) when one is momentarily uncertain of some point and seeks confirmation or (2) when one has remembered something. In the latter case, it is used with particular frequency when the speaker is fondly recalling something from the past. Despite its links to literary language, *-kke* is generally limited to casual spoken usage and should be avoided in formal situations.

(1) あしたの約束は6時だっけ。(TJ/MF)
*Ashita no yakusoku wa rokuji da**kke**.*
Our appointment tomorrow is for six o'clock, isn't it?

あしたの約束は6時だったっけ。(TJ/MF)
*Ashita no yakusoku wa rokuji datta**kke**.*
Our appointment tomorrow was for six o'clock, wasn't it?

あの人は誰だったっけ。(TJ/MF)
*Ano hito wa dare datta**kke**.*
Who was that person again?

(2) 子供の頃はいたずらしてよくしかられたっけ。(TJ/MF)
*Kodomo no koro wa itazura shite yoku shikarareta**kke**.*
When I was a kid, I remember I was always acting up and getting into trouble for this or that.

きょうは銀行はお休みだったっけ。うっかりしていたわ。
(TJ/F)
*Kyō wa ginkō wa oyasumi datta**kke**. Ukkari shite ita wa.*
Oh, that's right, today's a bank holiday! It had totally slipped my mind.

### • *Nakanaka* an adverb of degree, depending on context

The general meaning of this adverb is "more than is usual or expected," but the precise degree of intensity varies, as is also true of the very similar English term "rather." *Nakanaka* is close to *kanari* "pretty," "fairly," or *sōtō* "reasonably," "tolerably," and not usually as strong as *hijō ni* "extremely" or *totemo* "very much." However, it can also be used with a stronger nuance—when the speaker has in mind something like *zuibun*, *totemo* or *sugoku* ("considerably," "very," "terribly"), but prefers understatement. In this usage, the implicit meaning is actually very close to *totemo*.

この本はなかなかおもしろかったよ。(TJ/M)
*Kono hon wa **nakanaka** omoshirokatta yo.*
You know, this book was really rather interesting.

なかなか立派な息子さんでうらやましいですね。(NJ/MF)
***Nakanaka** rippa na musuko-san de urayamashii desu ne.*
You are lucky to have such a wonderful son.

## • *Shi* implies more to come

*Shi* is a conjunction which can be attached to the end of clauses and of sentences in order to imply that there is more which is not being said.

Two different usages are possible. (1) Trailing off, at the end of a subjective statement, with *shi* ("you know," "and everything") implies that there are numerous other reasons that would support your claim just as well. This is the form seen in the dialogue. (2) In addition, *shi* can be repeated at the end of every clause of a sentence, for emphasis.

(1) いろいろな話もできた**し**、今日は楽しかったわ。(TJ/F)

*Iroiro na hanashi mo dekita **shi**, kyō wa tanoshikatta wa.*

Today was a lot of fun. It was really great talking to you and stuff.

そろそろ会議を始めましょうか。定刻も過ぎていることです**し**。(NJ/MF)

*Sorosoro kaigi o hajimemashō ka. Teikoku mo sugite iru koto desu **shi**.*

Shall we begin the meeting now? We are already running behind schedule and all.

(2) 日当たりもいい**し**、駅から近い**し**、いい部屋を見つけたね。(TJ/M)

*Hiatari mo ii **shi**, eki kara chikai **shi**, ii heya o mitsuketa ne.*

It gets plenty of sun, it's close to the station—you've really found yourself a nice place!

頭は痛い**し**、寒気はする**し**、どうも風邪をひいたみたいなんです。(NJ/MF)

*Atama wa itai **shi**, samuke wa suru **shi**, dōmo kaze o hiita mitai nan desu.*

My head hurts and I've got the chills. I think I may be coming down with a cold.

# NECKTIE JAPANESE

Stefan Poggendorf, sales director in charge of Asia for the German company Theiss Pharmaceuticals, pays a visit to Masayuki Kubota, a new mid-level manager at one of Theiss's old clients, Nihon Pharmaceuticals. Mr. Poggendorf and Mr. Kubota have communicated by telephone and fax before, but this is their first face-to-face meeting.

**Poggendorf:** Good morning! How do you do? I'm Stefan Poggendorf, with Theiss Pharmaceuticals. (Presents his business card) I'm very happy to have this opportunity to meet with you.

**Kubota:** (Takes the card and offers his own) It's my pleasure. I'm Masayuki Kubota. (Motions toward a chair) Have a seat!

**Poggendorf:** Thank you.

**Kubota:** By the way, this must be the first time you've been here since we moved to our new office.

**Poggendorf:** Yes, it is. What a lovely place this is. You even have a marvelous view of Tokyo Bay.

**Kubota:** Yes, we were quite fortunate to find it.

## ネクタイ

ポゲンドルフ　おはようございます。本日はお忙しいところ、お時間をとっていただいて恐縮です。(名刺を差し出して)タイス製薬のポゲンドルフと申します。よろしくお願いいたします。

久保田　　　(名刺を受け取り、自分の名刺を差し出して)久保田で

ございます。よろしくお願いいたします。(椅子を示して)どうぞおかけください。

ポゲンドルフ 　恐れ入ります。

久保田 　ところで、私どもの新社屋にお越しいただいたのは初めてでしたでしょうか。

ポゲンドルフ 　はい、初めてです。なかなかいい所ですね。東京湾も見渡せますし。

久保田 　ええ、おかげさまで。

## NEKUTAI

**Pogendorufu:** *Ohayō gozaimasu. Honjitsu wa oisogashii tokoro, ojikan o totte itadaite kyōshuku desu. (Meishi o sashidashite) Taisu Seiyaku no Pogendorufu to mōshimasu. Yoroshiku onegai itashimasu.*

**Kubota:** *(Meishi o uketorinagara jibun no meishi o sashidashite) Kubota de gozaimasu. Yoroshiku onegai itashimasu. (Isu o shimeshite) Dōzo okake kudasai.*

**Pogendorufu:** *Osoreirimasu.*

**Kubota:** *Tokoro de, watakushi-domo no shin-shaoku ni okoshi itadaita no wa hajimete deshita deshō ka.*

**Pogendorufu:** *Hai, hajimete desu. Nakanaka ii tokoro desu ne. Tōkyō-wan mo miwatasemasu shi.*

**Kubota:** *Ee, okage-sama de.*

---

| NECKTIE NOTES |
| --- |

### • "Good Morning" in TJ and NJ

The Japanese equivalents of "Good afternoon" and "Good evening," *konnichiwa* and *konbanwa*, are used in both T-Shirt and Necktie Japanese, but the terms for "Good morning" vary according to the degree of formality. Among equals who are quite familiar, *ohayō gozaimasu* is contracted to *ohayō,* which is also used by superiors in addressing their subordinates.

● *Oisogashii tokoro*

*Oisogashii tokoro* (lit., "your busy time [place]") is a fixed Necktie Japanese phrase used to express gratitude for the hearer's time, efforts on one's behalf, etc. The Sino-Japanese equivalent is *gotabō no tokoro.* The question of whether the hearer is actually "busy" is less important than the need to show appreciation and deference.

> 本日は**お忙しいところ**、お集まりいただきまして誠にありがとうございました。(NJ/MF)
>
> *Honjitsu wa **oisogashii tokoro**, oatsumari itadakimashite makoto ni arigatō gozaimashita.*
>
> Thank you very much for taking time from your busy schedules to join us today.

> **お忙しいところ**すみませんが、あしたまでに来年度の予算案を提出していただけないでしょうか。(NJ/MF)
>
> ***Oisogashii tokoro*** *sumimasen ga, ashita made ni rainen-do no yosan-an o teishutsu shite itadakenai deshō ka.*
>
> I know you're busy and I'm sorry to trouble you, but do you think you could submit the budget for the coming fiscal year by tomorrow?

● **Deferential *o-* and *go-* before adjectives**

In Chapter 2, "At the Airport," we saw how deferential prefixes can be attached to nouns. Here we see that they can also appear before adjectives: *oisogashii* "busy," *outsukushii* "beautiful" and *oyasashii* "kind, gentle."

The feeling suggested is of respect for the hearer or referent. The prefix is much more likely to be attached to words that have a positive, pleasant meaning.

● *Tokoro:* **a point in time as well as space**

The Japanese *tokoro,* which usually means "place," coincides quite closely with the English word "point," since it too can be used to describe either time or space. *Tokoro* can be attached to verbs in their various forms in order to express the point just before, during or after something happens, as in *suru tokoro*, *shite iru tokoro* or *shita tokoro*. It can also be used with adjectives or verbs in their noun forms in polite phrases that describe the listener's frame of mind: *oisogashii tokoro* "when you're busy," *oyasumi no tokoro* "while you're resting (taking the day off)" and *otsukare no tokoro* "when you are tired."

(The point after something has happened: verb in the past tense)

今ちょうど帰ってきた**ところ**なんだ。(TJ/M)
*Ima chōdo kaette kita **tokoro** nan da.*
I just got home.

(The point when something is happening: verb in the *-te* form plus *iru*)

今、どうしようか考えている**ところ**です。(NJ/MF)
*Ima, dō shiyō ka kangaete iru **tokoro** desu.*
I'm just thinking about what I should do.

(The point before something happens: verb in the dictionary form)

これからそちらへうかがう**ところ**です。(NJ/MF)
*Kore kara sochira e ukagau **tokoro** desu.*
I'm just on my way to see you.

## • *Kyōshuku desu*

This Sino-Japanese compound literally refers to "shrinking" (*shuku*) from "fear" (*kyō*) and thus is close to the English "I'm afraid." An NJ expression, it is used in apologies and requests to express a solicitous, respectful attitude. It is usually interchangeable with the native Japanese *osoreirimasu*, but suggests a slightly higher degree of formality.

## • *Yoroshiku onegai itashimasu*

The nearly untranslatable phrase *yoroshiku onegai shimasu (itashimasu)* is very commonly used in introducing yourself or requesting favors from people you already know. The choice of *shimasu* or *itashimasu* is not crucial—both are within the realm of Necktie

Japanese—but *itashimasu*, being the humbler form, expresses the greater degree of deference.

### • *Humble verb forms o- ~ suru (itasu)*

Most verbs can be made into a humble form by adding *o-* in front of a verb's stem form, and *suru* or *itasu* following. These verb forms can only be used in regard to some activity of one's own which directly affects the listener, as in *onegai suru* "request (of you)," *owatashi suru* "deliver/hand over (to you)" or *o-okuri suru* "send (you)." In this way the speaker expresses respect for the beneficiary of the action.

When the verb is a Sino-Japanese compound, *go-* is usually substituted for *o-*, as in *gohōkoku suru* "report," "let you know," *gorenraku suru* "get in touch with you," *goannai suru* "show you around" and the like. However, there are some verbs which can take either the *o-* or the *go-* prefix, such as *ohenji suru (gohenji suru)* "respond."

The verb *suru*, or its humbler variant *itasu*, is normally used in these phrases in their more formal *-masu* form, as in *gohōkoku itashimasu* or *gorenraku itashimasu*.

Because the *o-* prefix is attached, it is easy to mistake this for an honorific form; however since it is humble it can in fact only be used to describe your own action, or that of someone in your in-group.

コーヒーのおかわりを**お持ちしましょう**か。(NJ/MF)
*Kōhii no okawari o **omochi shimashō** ka.*
Can I bring you a refill on your coffee?

何かありましたら**ご連絡します**。(NJ/MF)
*Nani ka arimashitara **gorenraku shimasu**.*
I will get in touch if anything should come up.

ただいま別の電話に出ておりますので、折り返しこちらから
**お電話いたします**。(NJ/MF)
*Tadaima betsu no denwa ni dete orimasu no de, orikaeshi kochira kara **odenwa itashimasu**.*
He (she) is on another line at the moment. He (she) will return your call (as soon as he/she finishes).

係りの者が**ご案内いたします**。(NJ/MF)

*Kakari no mono ga **goannai itashimasu***.

Someone from the appropriate department will be happy to escort you.

### • *Okake kudasai* "Have a seat"

Japanese *suwaru* "sit" has a broad range of meanings, but typically suggests sitting at ground level in traditional Japanese style, e.g., on tatami mats. Thus, when motioning toward a chair or sofa, you should say, instead of *osuwari kudasai*, *okake kudasai*. *Koshi kakeru* (lit., "perching one's backside") is used whenever you want to refer to sitting on a piece of furniture.

### • *Watashi* or *watakushi*

*Watakushi* is a formal, polite first-person pronoun used by men and women alike. It is written with the Chinese character which also means "private" or "personal": 私 *shi*. The contracted form *watashi* is nominally somewhat lower on the scale of formality and politeness, but has entered general usage as a less stiff, more colloquial variant. In fact, when encountering the Chinese character, many Japanese nowadays will read it simply as *watashi*.

In conversation with friends or intimates, men typically use the still more casual *boku* or *ore*. Since *ore* sounds very rough, it is used only among friends. Many women and some men use *atashi* but this sounds casual and a little rough.

### • *-Domo* as a plural suffix with nuances of humility

*-Domo* is a plural suffix with humble connotations. It is often attached, for instance, to the formal *watakushi* "I" to make the particular form of "we" (*watakushi-domo*) often used in business situations. It is almost always used in reference to oneself or one's in-group, not about others.

In *kodomo* "children," the suffix has become a permanent part of the word.

### • *Okoshi*—an honorific term for coming and going

*Okoshi* is a very formal and honorific term for "coming" or "going." It is formed from the verb *kosu* "cross, move." The phrase *okoshi ni naru* is often used to mean "come" or "go," as are *okoshi kudasaru* and *okoshi itadaku*; these last two are more polite because they contain a nuance of gratitude. As you will remember, *kudasaru* is the NJ equivalent of *kureru* ("do ~ for me") and *itadaku* the Necktie version of *morau* ("have someone do ~"). (For more information on *kureru* and *morau*, please see Chapters 2 and 3, pages 27 and 51.)

お近くにお越しの際は、どうぞお立ち寄りください。
  (NJ/MF)
*Ochikaku ni **okoshi** no sai wa, dōzo otachiyori kudasai.*
If you should be in the neighborhood, please stop by.

どちらへお越しですか? (NJ/MF)
*Dochira e **okoshi** desu ka?*
So you are off, then? (lit., "Where might you be going?")

わざわざお越しくださいまして、ありがとうございました。
  (NJ/MF)
*Wazawaza **okoshi** kudasaimashite, arigatō gozaimashita.*
Thank you for coming (troubling to come).


# EQUIVALENCY CHART

| T-SHIRT JAPANESE | NECKTIE JAPANESE |
|---|---|
| *Yā.* | *Ohayō gozaimasu.* |
| *Kyō wa* | *Honjitsu wa* |
| *isogashii no ni* | *oisogashii tokoro* |
| *jikan* | *ojikan* |
| *(-te) moratte* | *(-te) itadaite* |
| *sumanai ne.* | *kyōshuku desu.* |
| — | *~ de gozaimasu.* |
| *Yoroshiku.* | *Yoroshiku onegai itashimasu.* |
| *Mā suware yo.* | *Dōzo okake kudasai.* |
| *Dōmo.* | *Osoreirimasu.* |
| *uchi* | *watakushi-domo* |
| *atarashii ofisu* | *shin-shaoku* |

*kita*
*~ dattakke.*
*Un.*
*~ da ne.* (M)
*~ ru shi.*
*Mā ne.*

*okoshi itadaita*
*~ deshita deshō ka.*
*Hai, hajimete desu.*
*~ desu ne.*
*~ masu shi.*
*Ee, okage-sama de.*

# In the Dressing Room

試着室にて

## T-SHIRT JAPANESE

Michael Baldridge is enjoying a holiday in Hawaii with his girlfriend Minako. The two are planning a sailing trip for the next day, and have stopped in a local store to look for a light cotton jacket for Michael to wear on board.

**Michael:** (holding a jacket up in the mirror) Hmm, I wonder …

**Minako:** A bit subdued, but it's kind of nice.

**Michael:** Hmm, maybe so. How does the size look?

**Minako:** It's just the right length. The sleeves are a little long, but they'll do.

**Michael:** How about this one?

**Minako:** Now that's flashier. It seems to light up your entire face!

**Michael:** Is it *too* flashy?

**Minako:** Uh-uh. Both of them look fine on you, so now you're going to have to choose.

## Tシャツ

マイケル　（一着を当ててみて）どうかなあ。

美奈子　**ちょっと地味だけどいいんじゃない？**

マイケル　そうだね。サイズはどうだろう。

美奈子　丈はちょうどいいわね。袖がちょっと長めだけど、このくらいならいいと思うわ。

マイケル　（もう一着当ててみて）こっちはどう？

美奈子　こっちの方が派手よね。顔が明るく見えるわ。

マイケル　派手すぎるかな。

美奈子　ううん、別にそんなことないわよ。どっちも似合ってるから、好きな方にしたら？

## T-SHATSU

**Maikeru:** *(itchaku o atete mite) Dō ka nā.*

**Minako:** **Chotto jimi da kedo ii n' ja nai?**

**Maikeru:** *Sō da ne. Saizu wa dō darō.*

**Minako:** *Take wa chōdo **ii wa ne**. Sode ga **chotto nagame da kedo, kono kurai** nara ii to omou wa.*

**Maikeru:** *(mō itchaku o atete mite) **Kotchi** wa dō?*

**Minako:** *Kotchi no hō ga **hade yo ne**. Kao ga akaruku mieru wa.*

**Maikeru:** *Hade sugiru ka na.*

**Minako:** **Uun, betsu ni sonna koto nai wa yo. Dotchi mo niatte 'ru kara, suki na hō ni shitara?**

| T-SHIRT NOTES |

### • *Dō*—a "kosoado" word

*Dō* is one of the *kosoado* words which, you will remember, describe conditions.

The *kosoado* words include *kō* "this way," *sō* "that way," *ā* "that way" and *dō* "how." These terms are basically interchangeable with *kono yō ni*, *sono yō ni*, *ano yō ni* and *dono yō ni*. Of *kō*, *sō*, *ā* and *dō*, only *dō* always serves as a question.

*No* or *-nna* can also be added to the end of the *kosoado* adverbs to form related words, for instance, *kono hito* "this person" and *dono hito* "which person" or *konna hito* "this type of person" and *donna hito* "what sort of person." *Koko, soko, asoko* and *doko* all describe place or location, mainly in terms of how far away they are. And each of these series of words follows the same rules governing the use of the so-called *kosoado* words (for more information, please see Chapter 1, "Where Do I Change Trains," p. 16).

The word *dō* ("how," "in what way") can be used in five ways:

(1) The first is to express questions about content, circumstances or method:

> あの話はいったい**どう**なったんだろう。(TJ/M)
> *Ano hanashi wa ittai **dō** natta n' darō.*
> I wonder how the heck that story ever turned out.

> **どう**したらいいのか、自分でもわからないのよ。(TJ/F)
> ***Dō** shitara ii no ka, jibun de mo wakaranai no yo.*
> I don't have a clue what I should do.

(2) *Dō* can also be used when one has some questions or doubts but chooses to deny them and take a defiant stance:

> そんなことはもう**どう**でもいいわ。(TJ/F)
> *Sonna koto wa mō **dō** de mo ii wa.*
> It's all the same to me.

> **どう**にでもなれっていう心境だね。(TJ/M)
> ***Dō** ni de mo nare tte iu shinkyō da ne.*
> I couldn't care less how things turn out now.

(3) When *dō* is used in the phrases *dō ~-te mo* or *dō ~-tatte* it indicates that all the alternatives or options have been thoroughly considered:

> **どう**考え**ても**変だと思うんだ。(TJ/M)
> ***Dō** kangae**te mo** hen da to omou n' da.*
> No matter how you look at it, it's weird, I think.

> **どう**見**たって**、彼女は二十代にしか見えないわね。(TJ/F)
> ***Dō** mi**tatte**, kanojo wa nijū-dai ni shika mienai wa ne.*
> There's no way she looks older than twenty or so.

(4) *Dō* is also used to inquire about the listener's intention or circumstances, in proposals and other kinds of direct address (in many cases, *ikaga* can be used as a more polite variant).

お茶でも**どう**（いかが）ですか。(NJ/MF)
*Ocha de mo **dō** (ikaga) desu ka.*
Would you like some tea?

あなたは**どう**思う？(TJ/MF; here, *ikaga* would not be appropriate)
*Anata wa **dō** omou?*
What do you think?

(5) Finally, ~ *ka dō ka* corresponds to "whether or not":

そんなこと言った**かどうか**、忘れちゃったよ。(TJ/M)
*Sonna koto itta **ka dō ka**, wasurechatta yo.*
I can't remember if I said anything like that.

本当に彼が来る**かどうか**はわからないわよ。(TJ/F)
*Hontō ni kare ga kuru **ka dō ka** wa wakaranai wa yo.*
I don't know whether he'll actually come or not.

## • *Ka nā* used mostly by men

The sentence-final emphatic particle *ka na/ka nā* ("I wonder") can be used when talking to oneself, when asking an indirect question of the listener or when subtly promoting an idea and seeking agreement. It is typical of male speech; when it comes from young females, it has a slightly masculine ring. The complementary particle often used by women and which sounds feminine is *kashira*.

The form *ka nā* expresses stronger doubt than does *ka na*. The shorter and elongated forms alike can be used in any of several ways:

(1) To express the kind of doubt you might mutter aloud to yourself:

きょうの天気はどう**かな**。(TJ/M)
*Kyō no tenki wa dō **ka na**.*
I wonder what the weather's supposed to be like today.

忘れ物はない**かなあ**。(TJ/M)
*Wasuremono wa nai **ka nā**.*
I haven't forgotten anything, have I?

(2) To question the listener:

今から行って間に合う**かな**。(TJ/M)
*Ima kara itte maniau **ka na**.*
Do you think I'll make it if I leave now?

こんな時間に電話して迷惑じゃない**かなあ**。(TJ/M)
*Konna jikan ni denwa shite meiwaku ja nai **ka nā**?*
I wouldn't be bothering them if I were to phone at this hour,
    would I?

(3) To prod yourself into action, or solicit the listener's opinion:

たばこはもうやめよう**かな**。(TJ/M)
*Tabako wa mō yameyō **ka na**.*
Maybe I'll just quit smoking.

この本借りてもいい**かなあ**。(TJ/MF)
*Kono hon karite mo ii **ka nā**.*
I guess it's all right if I borrow this book.

(4) In negative constructions, it suggests a desire for something to
happen or come to be. In this usage, a close synonym is ~ *ni
nareba ii*. (See also the feminine equivalent *kashira* in Chapter 1,
p. 14.)

早く週末にならない**かな**。(TJ/M)
*Hayaku shūmatsu ni naranai **ka na**.*
I wish it was the weekend already!

困ったなあ。誰か来ない**かなあ**。(TJ/M)
*Komatta nā. Dare ka konai **ka nā**.*
Oh, shoot. Isn't anybody going to show up (and help)?

## • Being *jimi* (plain) is not necessarily a bad thing

The meaning of *jimi* [*na*] ranges from "drab" or "frumpy" to "un-
obtrusive" and "restrained." (Like other peoples, the Japanese
are sometimes ambivalent in their social and aesthetic ideals.)
Context will usually tell you whether the meaning is intended
negatively or positively. The opposite is *hade*.

その色は君にはちょっと**地味**だよ。(TJ/M)
*Sono iro wa kimi ni wa chotto **jimi** da yo.*
That color is a bit plain for you.

この洋服は**地味**ですがとても上品ですね。(NJ/MF)
*Kono yōfuku wa **jimi** desu ga totemo jōhin desu ne.*
This suit is on the conservative side, but it seems very elegant, doesn't it.

関口さんって、**地味だ**けど誠実な人よ。(TJ/F)
*Sekiguchi-san tte, **jimi da** kedo seijitsu na hito yo.*
Sekiguchi-san is kind of quiet, but she's very genuine.

年金生活だから**地味に**暮らしていますよ。(NJ/MF)
*Nenkin seikatsu da kara **jimi ni** kurashite imasu yo.*
We get by on just a pension, so we live quite modestly.

## • ~ *N' ja nai*: "Isn't it?"

*~ N' ja nai* is a T-Shirt phrase formed from *no de wa nai* by shortening *no* to *n'* and *de wa* to *ja*. In casual conversation, it is probably more commonly used than the unabbreviated form, *no de wa nai*.

寒い**んじゃない**かと思って、カーデガンを持ってきたわ。(TJ/F)
*Samui **n' ja nai** ka to omotte, kādegan o motte kita wa.*
I thought you might be cold, so I brought a cardigan.

この道、遠回り**なんじゃない**？(TJ/MF)
*Kono michi, tōmawari **nan ja nai**?*
Aren't we going the long way around, taking this route?

## • *Take* is used for length of clothing

*Take* is used to refer to vertical length, particularly when one is speaking of clothes, e.g., kimonos, skirts and trousers. The general word for length (of hair, rope, etc.) is *nagasa*. When talking about the height of trees, buildings, or diving boards, the appropriate word is *takasa*.

## • *Wa, wa ne* and *wa yo* have a feminine ring

These particles added to the ends of sentences are generally characteristic of female speech. They add an emotional, "soft" quality, and so are largely confined to informal speech.

*Wa* emphasizes the speaker's assertion, judgment, wish or

sense of surprise even as it softens the effect with a "feminine touch."

ねえ、見て。雪が降ってきたわ。(TJ/F)
*Nē, mite. Yuki ga futte kita **wa***.
Oh, look. It's snowing!

あなたに会えて本当にうれしかったわ。(TJ/F)
*Anata ni aete hontō ni ureshikatta **wa***.
I'm so happy I was able to see you.

*Wa ne* is similarly emphatic but also tends to seek agreement from the listener. *Wa ne* can also be used to express admiration, as in the second example below; when it is, *ne* is often lengthened to *nē*.

けさはずいぶん冷えるわね。(TJ/F)
*Kesa wa zuibun hieru **wa ne***.
It's really chilly this morning, isn't it?

恵里ちゃん、しばらく見ないうちにすっかり大きくなったわ
ねえ。(TJ/F)
*Eri-chan, shibaraku minai uchi ni sukkari ōkiku natta **wa nē***.
Eri, you've gotten so much bigger since the last time I saw you!

*Wa yo* is used to express one's opinion very definitely, in order to get the other person's attention or convince them of something. It is used almost exclusively by women; the male equivalent is *yo*.

お湯がわいてるわよ。(TJ/F)
*Oyu ga waite 'ru **wa yo***.
Oh, the water's boiling! (alternatively, this sentence can mean "Oh, the bath's ready [at a good temperature]").

あなたは気にしてるけど、ちっとも太ってないわよ。(TJ/F)
*Anata wa ki ni shite 'ru kedo, chitto mo futotte nai **wa yo***.
I know you're concerned about it, but you're not the least bit fat.

• *-Me* can be used as a suffix meaning "kind of"

*-Me* in combination with *naga-* ("long"), *mijika-* ("short") and *ō-*

(from *ōi* "much," "many"), etc. is a suffix meaning "somewhat" or "on the ... side."

このズボン、買ったときにはゆるめだと思ったけど、ちょうどよくなっちゃったよ。(TJ/M)

*Kono zubon, katta toki ni wa yurume da to omotta kedo, chōdo yoku natchatta yo.*

When I bought these trousers I thought they were a little loose, but now they're just right.

きょうは用事があるので早めに帰らせてください。(NJ/MF)

*Kyō wa yōji ga aru no de hayame ni kaerasete kudasai.*

Could I go home a little early today? There are some things I need to get done.

● *Kono kurai* means "this much"

As a noun, *kurai* means "grade," "rank," "position," but together with the *kosoado* adverbs *kono*, *sono*, *ano*, and *dono*, it is used as a quantifier: "much," "extent," "degree." The first consonant can be voiced, becoming *gurai*, as the speaker prefers. The form *kore kurai/gurai* is more or less interchangeable with *kono kurai/gurai*, although the former tends to suggest a broader range, a greater degree of approximation.

砂糖はこのくらいでいいかしら。(TJ/F)

*Satō wa **kono kurai** de ii kashira.*

I wonder whether this is the right amount of sugar.

このぐらいのけがならたいしたことないよ。(TJ/M)

***Kono gurai** no kega nara taishita koto nai yo.*

If the injury's only this bad, it's really nothing to worry about.

● *Kotchi, sotchi, atchi* and *dotchi*

*Kotchi, sotchi, atchi* and *dotchi* are the T-Shirt versions of the more formal *kochira, sochira, achira* and *dochira*. *Kotchi* and the other three terms usually refer to direction or place, though they can also be used in reference to people. (For example, *kotchi* means "here" and so by extension can also refer to "this side" or "me.") *Sotchi* means "there" (a short distance away), *atchi* "over there" (further away) and *dotchi* "where" (see also *kochira*, *sochira*, *achira* and *dochira* in Chapter 3, "Tied Up In a Meeting," page 57).

Four of the main uses of *kotchi* etc. are as follows:

(1) To guide the listener in a direction close to the speaker:

> こっちへ行こうよ。(TJ/M)
> *Kotchi e ikō yo.*
> Let's go this way.

> お手洗いはこっち（こちら）です。(TJ/MF)
> *Otearai wa **kotchi** (kochira) desu.*
> The restroom is this way.

(2) To describe things located in a spot close to the speaker, or to refer to that spot ("this place"/"here").

> こっちの方が安いし、いいんじゃない？(TJ/MF)
> *Kotchi no hō ga yasui shi, ii n' ja nai?*
> What about this one? It's cheaper and all.

> こっち（こちら）はまだ肌寒くてセーターがいるくらいです。
>   (NJ/MF)
> *Kotchi (kochira) wa mada hadasamukute sētā ga iru kurai
>   desu.*
> Here it still gets chilly enough that you need a sweater.

(3) To refer to people who are near to the speaker. "This person" is often used in introducing people to one another.

> 紹介するよ。こっちは山田さん、あっちは田中さんだ。
>   (TJ/M)
> *Shōkai suru yo. **Kotchi** wa Yamada-san, **atchi** wa Tanaka-san
>   da.*
> Let me introduce you. This is Yamada-san, and that's Tanaka-san.

(4) To refer to yourself or to your own "side" (point of view, etc.), as distinct from someone else's.

> こっちの気も知らないで、今までどこへ行ってたの？(TJ/F)
> *Kotchi no ki mo shiranai de, ima made doko e itte 'ta no?*
> Where have you been all this time? Don't you know how worried I was?

こっち（こちら）で必要な書類は用意しますので、印鑑をお願いします。(NJ/MF)

*Kotchi (kochira) de hitsuyō na shorui wa yōi shimasu no de, inkan o onegai shimasu.*

We will prepare the necessary documents here, so we will just need your signature seal (i.e., when you come in next time to pick up the papers).

• *Hade* [*na*] **typically has a negative connotation**

*Hade* [*na*] describes things that stand out or call attention to themselves. In Japan, perhaps because of the traditional view of humility as a virtue, it's always been considered safer not to stand out. So in most cases *hade* [*na*] is used either negatively or neutrally. It has three main uses:

(1) to describe eye-catching patterns, colors, ensembles and other visible things; (2) to refer to flamboyant personality traits or life-style choices; and (3) to mean "extremely," or describe something as being quite exaggerated.

(1) あのアロハシャツは派手で着られないよ。(TJ/M)
*Ano aroha shatsu wa **hade de** kirarenai yo.*
That Hawaiian shirt is too loud for me.

スポーツウェアは派手な色の方がいいんじゃありませんか。(NJ/MF)
*Supōtsu-ueā wa **hade na** iro no hō ga ii n' ja arimasen ka.*
Sportswear is supposed to be colorful and kind of flashy, don't you think?

(2) 彼女、外車を乗り回したりして、近頃急に派手になったわね。(TJ/F)
*Kanojo, gaisha o norimawashitari shite, chikagoro kyū ni **hade ni** natta wa ne.*
Don't you think she's suddenly begun acting a bit ostentatiously, riding around in that fancy foreign car and all?

忘年会は、ぱぁっと派手にやりましょう。(NJ/MF)
*Bōnen-kai wa, pātto **hade ni** yarimashō.*
Let's make the end-of-the-year party a real blowout, huh?

(3) あの子、ずいぶん派手に泣いてるけど、大丈夫かな。(TJ/M)
*Ano ko, zuibun **hade ni** naite 'ru kedo, daijōbu ka na.*

That kid is certainly putting on quite a show with her wailing. Do you think she's all right?

スキーに行って**派手に**転んじゃったんです。(NJ/MF)
*Sukii ni itte **hade ni** koronjatta n' desu.*
I went skiing and took a spectacular tumble.

## • *Betsu ni* is usually accompanied by a negative

*Betsu ni* is used in negative statements to mean "not particularly." It can be used by itself as a way of shrugging off or dismissing a question.

*Toku ni* and *tokubetsu ni* (both meaning "especially") can be used in either positive or negative constructions, whereas *betsu ni* is exclusively used in the latter.

**別に**用事はないのですが、どうなさっていらっしゃるかと思ってお電話しました。(NJ/MF)
***Betsu ni** yōji wa nai no desu ga, dō nasatte irassharu ka to omotte odenwa shimashita.*
It's nothing important. I just wondered how you were doing and thought I'd give you a call.

何かあったの？(TJ/MF)
*Nani ka atta no?*
Has something happened?
**別に**。(TJ/MF)
***Betsu ni.***
No, not really. (It's nothing./Nothing in particular.)

## • *-Nna* is somewhat more casual than *no yō na*

The *sonna* of the dialogue is one of the *kosoado* words that were first introduced in Chapter 1, "Where Do I Change Trains" (page 16). It is similar to *sono yō na* or *sō iu* (both meaning "that kind of") as well as *sore hodo* ("that much"). It is always followed by a noun. When words from the *konna* series precede verbs, adjectives or *na* adjectives, they are followed by *ni*, for *konna ni*, *sonna ni*, *anna ni* and *donna ni*. The particle *ni* is not attached, though, when these words precede nouns, as in the dialogue.

*Konna*, *sonna*, *anna* and *donna* can be used in both TJ and NJ, though the more formal equivalents are *kono yō na*, *sono yō na*, *ano yō na* and *dono yō na*.

きょうは早く帰ってきてね。(TJ/MF)
*Kyō wa hayaku kaette kite ne.*
Come home early tonight, okay, dear?

そんなこと言ったって、仕事だからわからないよ。(TJ/M)
***Sonna** koto itta tte, shigoto da kara wakaranai yo.*
Sure, sure. You know I've got a job to do and can't make any
  promises.

そんなに急いでどちらへいらっしゃるんですか。(NJ/MF)
***Sonna ni** isoide dochira e irassharu n' desu ka.*
Where are you off to in such a big hurry?

## • *-Te iru* is often abbreviated as *-te 'ru*

In spoken Japanese, the *-te iru* form of verbs is contracted to *-te 'ru*
by dropping the "*i*" for the sake of speed and fluidity. The same
thing happens with *-de iru* verbs, which of course become *-de 'ru*.

知ってるよ。(TJ/M)
*Shitte 'ru yo.*
I know that!

子どもたち道路で遊んでるのよ。危ないわ。(TJ/F)
*Kodomo-tachi dōro de asonde 'ru no yo. Abunai wa.*
The kids are playing in the street. That can't be very safe.

# NECKTIE JAPANESE

Michael Baldridge is in a department store dressing room, trying on tuxedos. With his friend's wedding just one week away, he hopes to decide on a tux today.

**Baldridge:** (trying one on) Hmm, I don't know …

**Clerk:** Quite chic, I'd say.

**Baldridge:** Hmm, maybe so. What do you think of the fit?

**Clerk:** The length is just right, sir. The sleeves seem a little bit long, but not so much that they would need to be altered.

**Baldridge:** (trying on a different one) How about this one?

**Clerk:** Well now, that certainly has some flair to it. It really brings out your features.

**Baldridge:** You mean it's a bit overdone, then?

**Clerk:** Oh, I wouldn't say that! Both are very flattering. The decision, of course, is entirely yours.

## ネクタイ

ボルドリッジ　（試着して）どうかなあ。

販売員　　　**シックな感じでおよろしいんじゃございませんか。**

ボルドリッジ　そうだね。サイズはどうだろう。

販売員　　　**着丈の方はちょうどよろしゅうございますね。お袖が気持ち長めでしょうか。この程度ならお直しの必要もないと思いますが。**

ボルドリッジ　（もう一着を試着して）こっちはどう？

| 販売員 | こちらの方が華やかな感じですね。お顔うつりもよろしゅうございます。 |
|---|---|
| ボルドリッジ | 派手すぎるかな。 |
| 販売員 | いいえ、そのようなことは決してございません。どちらもよくお似合いでございます。あとはお客様のお好みで選んでいただいた方が……。 |

## NEKUTAI

**Borudorijji:** *(shichaku shite) Dō ka nā.*

**Hanbai-in:** *Shikku na kanji de oyoroshii n' ja gozaimasen ka.*

**Borudorijji:** *Sō da ne. Saizu wa dō darō.*

**Hanbai-in:** *Kitake no hō wa chōdo yoroshū gozaimasu ne. Osode ga kimochi nagame deshō ka. Kono teido nara onaoshi no hitsuyō mo nai to omoimasu ga.*

**Borudorijji:** *(mō itchaku o shichaku shite) Kotchi wa dō?*

**Hanbai-in:** *Kochira no hō ga hanayaka na kanji desu ne. Okao-utsuri mo yoroshū gozaimasu.*

**Borudorijji:** *Hade sugiru ka na.*

**Hanbai-in:** *Iie, sono yō na koto wa kesshite gozaimasen. Dochira mo yoku oniai de gozaimasu. Ato wa okyaku-sama no okonomi de erande itadaita hō ga …*

---

### NECKTIE NOTES

• **The customer is always right**

When dealing with customers or clients, Japanese are generally extremely deferential. Store clerks and bank tellers are often particularly so. Bank employees, especially, are likely to use *-sama* when addressing customers, and *gozaimasu* in place of *desu*.

There is no need for the customer to respond with equal

politeness or deference. Ordinary day-to-day forms, whether *desu/ -masu* or the T-Shirt *da*, suffice.

Generally, the speech style used by sellers of day-to-day necessities is close to TJ; those who lay on the honorifics are more likely to be purveyors of more expensive items—luxury goods or anything with a degree of snob appeal.

### • *Shikku na kanji* suggests refinement

The French/English word "chic" has been borrowed and made a part of the Japanese language (*shikku [na]*). Like the native Japanese *iki*, *shikku* suggests sophistication without ostentation, while avoiding the connotations of dullness attached to *jimi* ("subdued"). The clerk in the dialogue is careful to use unambiguously complimentary language while, at the same time, avoiding laying on the praise too thick for fear of sounding insincere. The clerk here strikes a good balance with ~ *kanji* "a feeling of ~," "a certain ~."

### • *Yoroshii, yoi* and *ii*

*Yoi* is one term which can be used to describe situations that are desirable or pleasing, but is largely confined to written language. In spoken Japanese, the more casual pronunciation *ii* is more common.

*Yoroshii* often substitutes in more Necktie conversations, and has the same meaning of "good," "suitable" or "satisfactory." It is often followed by *gozaimasu*, and when it is, the pronunciation changes, becoming *yoroshū*.

### • *No hō* can be used for polite indirectness

The word *hō* is most commonly used in discussions of physical direction or location, but is also often used in any of several other ways:

(1) to describe one party to, or opponent in, a negotiation, business deal or other transaction;

(2) to compare one a person or object to another;

(3) to describe a person as more or less having certain qualities; and finally, by extension from these,

(4) to avoid precision and bluntness in a context where politeness is called for.

In particular, this last usage is often employed by store clerks and businesspeople as a way of expressing deference while also maintaining some psychological distance from the customer.

(1) 中田先生の**方**から電話がかかってきて、あわてちゃったわ。(TJ/F)

*Nakada sensei no **hō** kara denwa ga kakatte kite, awatechatta wa.*

We got an unexpected call from Professor Nakada's office, and I got all flustered!

こちらの**方**こそお世話になっております。(NJ/MF)

*Kochira no **hō** koso osewa ni natte orimasu.*

No, no, we are the ones (I am the one) who should be thanking you.

(2) 大きい**方**を君にあげるよ。(TJ/M)

*Ōkii **hō** o kimi ni ageru yo.*

You can have the bigger one.

妹の**方**が私よりずっと背が高いんです。(NJ/MF)

*Imōto no **hō** ga watashi yori zutto se ga takai n' desu.*

My sister's a lot taller than me.

(3) こう見えても気が小さい**方**なんだ。(TJ/M)

*Kō miete mo ki ga chiisai **hō** nan da.*

Maybe you wouldn't think so, but I'm actually kind of on the timid side.

高橋さんは夜よく寝られる**方**ですか。(NJ/MF)

*Takahashi-san wa yoru yoku nerareru **hō** desu ka.*

Are you able to sleep pretty well at night, Mr. Takahashi?

(4) お仕事の**方**はいかがですか？(NJ/MF)

*Oshigoto no **hō** wa ikaga desu ka?*

How are things at work?

コーヒーにミルクの**方**はお入れしますか？(NJ/MF)

*Kōhii ni miruku no **hō** wa oire shimasu ka?*

Do you take milk in your coffee?

- *Kimochi* can mean "just a bit"

When *kimochi* is used as a noun it refers to one's heart or feelings, but when used as an adverb it refers to degree: "just a bit," "somewhat."

In both these cases, the similar word *kokoromochi* acts as a synonym. Both terms tend to suggest that the speaker is a bit of a stickler or overly sensitive.

あそこに掛かってる絵、**気持ち**左が下がってると思わない？ (TJ/MF)

*Asoko ni kakatte 'ru e, **kimochi** hidari ga sagatte 'ru to omowanai?*

Don't you think that painting over there is tilted just a hair down toward the left?

前髪は**気持ち**短めに切ってください。(NJ/MF)

*Maegami wa **kimochi** mijikame ni kitte kudasai.*

Could you cut the bangs a little bit on the short side?

- *Hanayaka na kanji* is gorgeous, not gaudy

*Hanayaka* [*na*] expresses the idea that something is bright, conspicuous and beautiful. It can be used to describe things which are luxurious, sumptuous or magnificent.

*Hade* [*na*] ("flashy"), as we have already seen, carries some negative connotations, and so when the speaker wishes to express unambiguous praise, he or she might better use *hanayaka* [*na*].

きのうのオペラには**華やかな**服装の人が大勢いましたね。 (NJ/MF)

*Kinō no opera ni wa **hanayaka na** fukusō no hito ga ōzei imashita ne.*

At the opera yesterday, there certainly were a lot of people dressed in rich, sumptuous clothes, weren't there?

- *Okao-utsuri mo yoroshū gozaimasu*

The clerk is using the most deferential language here. In concrete terms, he or she is saying that the color and pattern of this tuxedo enhance the customer's facial features nicely.

# EQUIVALENCY CHART

| T-SHIRT JAPANESE | NECKTIE JAPANESE |
| --- | --- |
| *Chotto jimi da kedo* | *Shikku na kanji de* |
| *ii n' ja nai?* | *oyoroshii n' ja gozaimasen ka.* |
| *~ wa* | *~ no hō wa* |
| *ii wa ne.* (F) | *yoroshū gozaimasu ne.* |
| *sode* | *osode* |
| *chotto* | *kimochi* |
| *nagame da kedo,* | *nagame deshō ka.* |
| *kono kurai* | *Kono teido* |
| *kotchi* | *Kochira* |
| *hade* | *hanayaka na kanji* |
| *~ yo ne.* | *~ desu ne.* |
| *Kao ga akaruku mieru wa.* | *Okao-utsuri mo yoroshū gozaimasu.* |
| *Uun,* | *Iie,* |
| *betsu ni sonna koto nai wa yo.* (F) | *sono yō na koto wa kesshite gozaimasen.* |
| *Dotchi* | *Dochira* |
| *niatte 'ru kara,* | *yoku oniai de gozaimasu.* |
| *suki na hō ni shitara?* | *Ato wa okyaku-sama no oko-nomi de erande itadaita hō ga ...* |

# Parents and Children's Fitness Day

## 子供の運動会

## T-SHIRT JAPANESE

André Bartsch works for Fuji Glass. During a lunchbreak, he chats with his colleague, Takafumi Ōsawa.

**Takafumi:** I tell you, my son's school had its parents and children's fitness day yesterday. I must have gone a little overboard, because I sure am feeling it today.

**André:** How old is your son?

**Takafumi:** He's in fifth grade. I don't know which one of us he takes after, but he's full of the devil.

**André:** So, what contest were you in?

**Takafumi:** The bread-eating contest.* My legs were killing me and I had started out the day with a hangover, too. It was awful, I tell you. And the wife was over on the sidelines yelling "Go for it!" at the top of her lungs and getting the whole thing on video, for Pete's sake.

**André:** You know, Takafumi, for a minute there I almost thought I detected a note of self-satisfaction in your voice. Well, at home, anyhow, it's pretty clear that you're a real go-getter.

**Takafumi:** Now wait a minute, what's *that* supposed to mean, "at home"?

* Races in which contestants must stop periodically on the way to the finish line to eat pieces of bread dangling from strings. Contestants are not allowed to touch the bread with their hands.

# Tシャツ

隆文 いやあ、きのう子供の運動会ではりきっちゃった もんだから、あちこちが痛くて。参ったなあ。

アンドレ 子供さんはいくつなの?

隆文 小学校5年生。誰に似たのか、こいつが腕白で腕白 で。

アンドレ で、どの競技に出たの?

隆文 パン食い競争。足はつりそうになるわ、二日酔い だわでひどいめにあっちゃったよ。女房は「パパ ー!」なんて金切り声を張り上げながらビデオを回 すしさ。

アンドレ でも、大沢さん、満更でもなさそうだよ。うちで は大活躍なんだね。

隆文 おいおい、「うちでは」ってどういう意味だよ。


# T-SHATSU

**Takafumi:** *Iyā, kinō kodomo no undō-kai de harikitchatta mon da kara, achi-kochi ga itakute. Maitta nā.*

**Andore:** **Kodomo-san** *wa* **ikutsu na no?**

**Takafumi:** *Shōgakkō gonen-sei. Dare ni nita no ka, koitsu ga wanpaku de wanpaku de.*

**Andore:** **De**, *dono kyōgi ni* **deta no?**

**Takafumi:** *Pankui kyōsō. Ashi wa tsurisō ni naru wa, futsuka-yoi da wa de hidoi me ni atchatta yo. Nyōbō wa "Papā!" nante kanakiri-goe o hariagenagara bideo o mawasu shi sa.*

**Andore:** *Demo,* **Ōsawa-san,** *manzara de mo nasasō* **da yo. Uchi** *de wa dai-katsuyaku* **nan da ne.**

**Takafumi:** *Oioi, "uchi de wa" tte dō iu imi da yo.*

### • *Iyā* is a common male interjection

The interjection *iya*, also elongated as *iyā*, expresses surprise or amazement. It is used mostly by men. A similar but somewhat stronger version is *iya mō*.

いや、驚いたよ。平日の昼間なのに映画館が満員なんだ。(TJ/M)

*Iya, odoroita yo. Heijitsu no hiruma na no ni eiga-kan ga man-in nan da.*

Now, that's a surprise! Imagine the movie theater being completely packed on a weekday!

いやあ、ほんとうに山の空気は気持ちいいですね。(NJ/MF)

*Iyā, hontō ni yama no kūki wa kimochi ii desu ne.*

Boy, mountain air sure is refreshing, isn't it?

いやもう、あんまりひどい渋滞なのであきれましたよ。(NJ/M)

*Iya mō, anmari hidoi jūtai na no de akiremashita yo.*

Gee, what a horrible traffic jam! Unbelievable!

### • *Mon da kara* explains why

*Mon da kara* is the casual contraction of *mono da kara*. It is an explanatory phrase, tacked onto the end of statements of reasons why something happened. The NJ equivalent is *mono desu kara*. The T-Shirt and Necktie versions alike can follow either verbs or adjectives.

There is no substantial difference in meaning between this phrase and the explanatory phrases *da kara* or *na no de*.

ゆうべ夜更かししちゃった**もんだから**、眠くて、眠くて。(TJ/MF)

*Yūbe yo-fukashi shichatta **mon da kara**, nemukute, nemukute.*

Last night I was up really late, and now I'm practically dead on my feet!

なにぶん急なお話だった**ものですから**、驚いてしまいました。(NJ/MF)

*Nani-bun kyū na ohanashi datta **mono desu kara**, odoroite shimaimashita.* (NJ/MF)

In any event, the matter came up so suddenly that I was quite surprised.

## • *Achi-kochi:* here, there and everywhere

*Achi-kochi* and its variants *atchi-kotchi* and *achira-kochira* are comparable to the English set expressions "all over (the place)," "everywhere" and "high and low."

Their order of formality is as follows:

| | |
|---|---|
| *atchi-kotchi* | casual |
| *achi-kochi* | formal and casual |
| *achira-kochira* | formal |

あっちこっち探したけれど、どうしてもうちの鍵が見つからないんだ。(TJ/M)

***Atchi-kotchi*** *sagashita keredo, dōshite mo uchi no kagi ga mitsukaranai n' da.*

I've looked high and low for my house key, but I just can't find it.

京都ならあちこち歩き回っていますから、よく知っていますよ。(NJ/MF)

*Kyōto nara **achi-kochi** arukimawatte imasu kara, yoku shitte imasu yo.*

I've walked all over Kyoto, so I know it quite well.

## • *Maitta* an admission of human frailty

*Maitta* is the past-tense form of *mairu*, the humble word for "go," "come," "call upon." The use of *mairu* as an exclamation expresses dismay, embarrassment, defeat or utter fatigue. It tends to be more typical of male than of female speech.

In sports, notably the martial arts, a contender may say *maitta!* when conceding defeat to an opponent. In general usage, it often means simply that you can't cope with or stand something.

こう暑い日が続くと体が参ってしまうね。(TJ/M)

*Kō atsui hi ga tsuzuku to karada ga **maitte** shimau ne.*

With one hot day after another like this, it gets to you, doesn't it?

お父さんのせっかちには**参る**わね。(TJ/F)

*Otōsan no sekkachi ni wa **mairu** wa ne.*

Isn't it amazing how Father always manages to run around like a chicken with its head cut off?

実は深夜のいたずら電話に**参って**いるんです。(NJ/MF)

*Jitsu wa shin'ya no itazura denwa ni **maitte** iru n' desu.*

Actually, we've been getting these annoying crank phone calls in the middle of the night.

きのうの大雨には**参りました**。電車が止まってしまったんですから。(NJ/MF)

*Kinō no ōame ni wa **mairimashita**. Densha ga tomatte shimatta n' desu kara.*

Yesterday's rainstorm was so bad that the trains stopped running, which left me in a real bind.

● *Nā* is a men's T-Shirt phrase

*Nā* (or its shorter variant *na*) is used primarily by men in casual speech. Though it is now also heard among younger women, it still has a somewhat gruff, masculine ring to it. The longer *nā* suggests more intense feeling. This particle usually appears at the end of sentences, in any of four different ways: (1) emotive, expressing joy, sadness or regret; (2) expressive of hope or desire; (3) affirmative, conveying a judgment or opinion; (4) solicitous, seeking the listener's agreement. In the first three usages, the corresponding feminine particle is *wa*; in the fourth, the equivalent would be *ne* or *wa ne*.

(1) きょうはいい天気だ**な**。(TJ/M)

*Kyō wa ii tenki da **na**.*

The weather's great today!

きのうのうちに準備しておけばよかった**なあ**。(TJ/M)

*Kinō no uchi ni junbi shite okeba yokatta **nā**.*

I should've had everything ready yesterday.

(2) 早く風邪が治るといい**な**。(TJ/M)

*Hayaku kaze ga naoru to ii **na**.*

I hope I get over this cold soon.

来年こそは家を買いたい**なあ**。(TJ/M)

*Rainen koso wa ie o kaitai **nā**.*
I sure hope I'll be able to buy a house next year, anyway.

(3) 夕飯までにきっと腹がへると思う**な**。(TJ/M)
*Yūhan made ni kitto hara ga heru to omou **na**.*
I think we'll be hungry by suppertime, for sure!

日曜日の朝早くから出かけるなんて、いやだ**なあ**。(TJ/M)
*Nichiyōbi no asa hayaku kara dekakeru nante, iya da **nā**.*
I *hate* the idea of getting up early to go out on a Sunday!

(4) ようやく朝晩涼しくなってきた**な**。(TJ/M)
*Yōyaku asaban suzushiku natte kita **na**.*
The mornings and evenings are finally getting cooler, huh?

疲れた**なあ**。ひと休みしようよ。(TJ/M)
*Tsukareta **nā**. Hitoyasumi shimashō yo.*
Oh, I'm really tired. Let's take a break.

## • Courtesy even among close friends

The need to distinguish "my family" from "your family" is part of
the general pattern of the in-group/out-group distinction in Japanese society. Even in T-Shirt contexts, a habit of expressing respect
for other people's families is basic. People refer to their own family members without any honorifics, but use a note of deference
when referring to relatives of even their close friends. When you
are speaking Necktie Japanese to a member of your out-group,
you must attach either *-san* or the even more polite *-sama*. There
is one irregular form: *kodomo* becomes *kodomo-san* or *okosan* or,
in an even more polite form, *okosama*.

| in-group | out-group |
|---|---|
| *kodomo* my children | *kodomo-san, okosan, okosama* your (his/her/their) child(ren) |
| *shujin* my husband | *goshujin* your (her) husband |
| *kanai* my wife | *okusan* your (his) wife |
| *imōto* my younger sister | *imōto-san* your (his/her/their) younger sister |
| *otōto* my younger brother | *otōto-san* your (his/her/their) younger brother |
| *ane* my older sister | *onēsan* your (his/her/their) older sister |

| | |
|---|---|
| *ani* my older brother | *oniisan* your (his/her/their) older brother |
| *haha* my mother | *okāsan* your (his/her/their) mother |
| *chichi* my father | *otōsan* your (his/her/their) father |
| *oya, ryōshin* my parents | *goryōshin* your (his/her/their) parents |

In TJ, males frequently refer to their parents as *ofukuro* "my mother" and *oyaji* "my father." In casual speech, they may refer to their friends' parents as *ofukuro-san* "your mother" and *oyaji-san* "your father."

*Haha* and *chichi* are neutral, formal words you use for your own parents when speaking to people in your out-group. You would never use these terms in direct address, nor to refer to anybody else's parents. Other people's parents are generally *okāsan* and *otōsan*. And finally, to make things really complicated, you can use *okāsan* and *otōsan*, or the variants *kāsan* and *tōsan*, in direct address to your parents, or in third-person reference to them when you speak with close friends.

### • *Koitsu, soitsu, aitsu, doitsu*

These terms are used, most often by men, for both people and objects; in other words, they may correspond to either *kono hito*, *sono hito*, *ano hito* and *dono hito*. When they are used to indicate people, the meaning is deprecatory—in many cases, overtly hostile or contemptuous (1). In some contexts, however, the speaker's intention is affectionate irony (2). But it is best to exercise care when using these forms for either purpose, since they sound masculine, rough and slangy.

(1) こいつがおれの財布を盗もうとしたんだ。(TJ/M)
*Koitsu ga ore no saifu o nusumō to shita n' da.*
This creep tried to steal my wallet.

そいつの言うことは真っ赤なうそだ。(TJ/M)
*Soitsu no iu koto wa makka na uso da.*
Everything he says is an out-and-out lie!

何もかもあいつが悪いんだ。(TJ/M)
*Nani mo kamo aitsu ga warui n' da.*
Anyway, it's all his (her) fault!

こんないたずらをしたのはいったいどこのどいつだ。(TJ/M)
*Konna itazura o shita no wa ittai doko no doitsu da.*

Who's the wise guy who would have pulled a trick like this?

(2) **こいつ**、見かけによらずかわいいところがあるんだぜ。
    (TJ/M)
   *Koitsu, mikake ni yorazu kawaii tokoro ga aru n' da ze.*
   Ya know, she may not look like much, but there's something
   sort of cute about her.

   **そいつ**のおやじさんが夕べひょっこり訪ねてきてね。(TJ/M)
   *Soitsu no oyaji-san ga yūbe hyokkori tazunete kite ne.*
   Last night, his dad suddenly showed up, you know?

   **あいつ**、今頃どうしてるだろう。(TJ/M)
   *Aitsu, imagoro dō shite 'ru darō.*
   I wonder what old what's-her-name is up to these days.

   大学のクラブの連中は**どいつ**もいいやつばかりなんだ。
    (TJ/M)
   *Daigaku no kurabu no renchū wa **doitsu** mo ii yatsu bakari
    nan da.*
   The members of the university club are a bunch of really great
    guys!

(3) **こいつ**はうまいよ。君もひとつどうだい。(TJ/M)
   *Koitsu wa umai yo. Kimi mo hitotsu dō dai.*
   This one's really tasty. Why don't you try one?

   **そいつ**は驚いたね。(TJ/M)
   *Soitsu wa odoroita ne.*
   Wow, that's really surprising.

   **あいつ**より**こいつ**の方が軽くて便利だぜ。(TJ/M)
   *Aitsu yori **koitsu** no hō ga karukute benri da ze.*
   This one's lighter and easier to use than that one.

   **どいつ**でもいいから、好きなのを持っていけよ。おまえにや
    るよ。(TJ/M)
   *Doitsu de mo ii kara, suki na no o motte ike yo. Omae ni yaru
    yo.*
   I don't care. Take whichever one you like. It's yours.

## • Starting sentences with *de*

*De* can be used at the beginning of sentences as a contracted form of phrases including *soko de* "at that point," *sore de* "so then" or *sō iu wake de* "that being the case." It is used (1) to encourage your conversational partner to continue speaking or (2) to mark the beginning of a statement that clarifies or explains what one has just said. In both these senses, it is comparable to the English "so."

*De* is used in speech ranging from casual to fairly formal, but is not appropriate in extremely formal situations.

(1) きのう、川久保さんに久しぶりに電話したんだ。(TJ/M)
*Kinō, Kawakubo-san ni hisashiburi ni denwa shita n' da.*
I telephoned Kawakubo-san yesterday for the first time in ages.
で、彼女、元気だった? (TJ/MF)
*De, kanojo, genki datta?*
So, how was she?

ただ今、故障で電車が止まっております。(NJ/MF)
*Tadaima, koshō de densha ga tomatte orimasu.*
Train service is stopped for a moment due to a malfunction.
で、いつ動くんですか? (NJ/MF)
*De, itsu ugoku n' desu ka?*
So when is it going to start up again?

(2) 帰ってきたらドアに鍵がかかっているのよ。で、仕方がない から外で待ってたの。(TJ/F)
*Kaette kitara doa ni kagi ga kakatte iru no yo. De, shikata ga nai kara soto de matte 'ta no.*
I get home, see, and the door's locked. So I have no choice but to wait outside.

実は10月に結婚するんです。で、披露宴にぜひ来ていただき たいんですが。(NJ/MF)
*Jitsu wa jūgatsu ni kekkon suru n' desu. De, hirō-en ni zehi kite itadakitai n' desu ga.*
Actually, I'm getting married in October. And see, I'd really like you to come to the reception.

## • Consecutive interjections … *wa*, … *wa*

We noted earlier that the particle *wa* when used at the end of sentences and pronounced with a rising intonation is a quintessential mark of feminine speech, to be avoided by males.

There is, however, another pattern, used by men and women, in which the *wa* is repeated, and spoken with a falling intonation. Used consecutively, it indicates emphasis, surprise or dismay (compare also *shi*, page 84).

せっかくの旅行だったのに、歯は痛くなる**わ**、おなかはこわすわでさんざんでした。(NJ/MF)

*Sekkaku no ryokō datta no ni, ha wa itaku naru **wa**, onaka wa kowasu **wa** de sanzan deshita.*

I'd gone away on holiday but wound up having a wretched time, what with first getting a toothache and then having my stomach act up.

さとる君、細いのに食べる**わ**、食べる**わ**、もうびっくりしたよ。(TJ/M)

*Satoru-kun, hosoi no ni taberu **wa**, taberu **wa**, mō bikkuri shita yo.*

Satoru-kun is thin as a rail, but when I saw the way he eats and eats, I was amazed.

● *Hidoi* and *sugoi*

The adjective *hidoi* derives from Sino-Japanese *hidō*, originally a Buddhist term for "injustice" (lit., "contrary to the Way"). *Hidoi* is common in colloquial speech. (1) It can be used for very negative descriptions of behavior: "cruel," "mean," "outrageous," "inhuman." (2) It can also be used to describe things which fail to satisfy: "bad (-tasting/-looking)" "nasty," "horrible." (3) And finally, like the English "terrible," *hidoi* can be used as a simple intensifier.

(1) いくらなんでも**ひど**すぎないか。あそこまで子供をしからなくてもいいのに。(TJ/M)

*Ikura nan-demo **hido**suginai ka. Asoko made kodomo o shikaranakute mo ii no ni.*

Haven't you gone a little too far? There's no need to scold a child *that* harshly.

きのうは**ひどい**ことを言ってしまってすみませんでした。(NJ/MF)

*Kinō wa **hidoi** koto o itte shimatte sumimasen deshita.*

I said some terrible things yesterday and I'm sorry.

(2) **ひどい**料理だったなあ。まずくて食べられなかったよ。
   (TJ/M)
   *Hidoi ryōri datta nā. Mazukute taberarenakatta yo.*
   The food was wretched! It was so bad I couldn't eat it.

   今学期は**ひどい**成績だっだので、来学期は頑張りたいと思い
   ます。(NJ/MF)
   *Kongakki wa **hidoi** seiseki datta no de, raigakki wa ganbaritai
   to omoimasu.*
   My marks this term were really bad, so next term I'm going to
   work hard (to improve them).

(3) **ひどく**落ち込んでいるみたいだけど、何かあったの? (TJ/MF)
   *Hidoku ochikonde iru mitai da kedo, nani ka atta no?*
   You seem awfully down. Is there something wrong?

   **ひどい**雨ですね。タクシーひろいましょうか。(NJ/MF)
   *Hidoi ame desu ne. Takushii hiroimashō ka.*
   It's raining like a son of a gun. What do you say we get a cab?

The original meaning of *sugoi* is "uncanny," "monstrous,"
"terrifying" (1). Unlike *hidoi*, it has, in modern colloquial speech,
developed the positive meaning of "extraordinary," "marvelous"
(2). The adverbial form *sugoku* functions very much like the English term "awfully," that is, as a simple intensifier used without
much thought given to the original sense of the word (3).

(1) さっきはほんとうに怖かったよ。**すごい**顔でにらむんだもの。
   (TJ/M)
   *Sakki wa hontō ni kowakatta yo. **Sugoi** kao de niramu n' da
   mono.*
   You really scared me a while ago. That was a pretty horrible
   glare you gave me.

   下を見たら**すごい**絶壁で足がすくみました。(NJ/MF)
   *Shita o mitara **sugoi** zeppeki de ashi ga sukumimashita.*
   I took one look down off the edge of that cliff and could feel
   my knees (almost start to) buckle.

(2) あの人、**すごい**家に住んでいるのよ。昔からの資産家らしい
   わ。(TJ/F)
   *Ano hito, **sugoi** uchi ni sunde iru no yo. Mukashi kara no
   shisan-ka rashii wa.*

He lives in a house you wouldn't believe! Apparently his family has money from way back.

**すごい**ですね。とても子供の絵とは思えません。(NJ/MF)
*Sugoi desu ne. Totemo kodomo no e to wa omoemasen.*
That picture is really something. You would never think that a child drew it.

(3) 眼鏡を変えたら**すごく**よく見えるようになったわ。(TJ/F)
*Megane o kaetara **sugoku** yoku mieru yō ni natta wa.*
Getting new glasses has improved my vision tremendously.

週末だったせいか、デパートは**すごい**混雑でした。(NJ/MF)
*Shūmatsu datta sei ka, depāto wa **sugoi** konzatsu deshita.*
Maybe it was because it was a weekend, but the department store was terribly crowded.

### • *Me* can refer to painful or dramatic experiences

The set phrase, "(adjective) + *me ni au*" means "to have a certain type of unpleasant experience." *Hidoi me ni au* means to "have a horrible experience." Similar phrases include *abunai me ni au* "have a close scrape," *tonde mo nai me ni au* "have an absurd time of it," *sanzan na me ni au* "have a harrowing ordeal" and *itai me ni au* "have a bitter experience."

ニューヨークは危ないとよく言われるけど、**怖いめにあった**ことは一度もないよ。(TJ/M)
*Nyū Yōku wa abunai to yoku iwareru kedo, **kowai me ni atta** koto wa ichido mo nai yo.*
They often say New York is dangerous, but I've never had anything scary happen to me.

今のうちに治療しておかないと、あとで**痛いめに合う**ことになりますよ。(NJ/MF)
*Ima no uchi ni chiryō shite okanai to, ato de **itai me ni au** koto ni narimasu yo.*
If you don't get this (medical problem) taken care of, you'll really suffer for it later!

### • *Sa* as a T-Shirt particle which adds emphasis

*Sa* is a T-Shirt particle added to the end of sentences and the end of clauses. It can be attached to verbs, nouns and adjectives. Its usage is especially heavy in the Tokyo-Kanto area, where it sometimes appears in almost every phrase:

きのうさ、デパートに行ったんだけどさ、欲しい物がなくてさ、結局何も買わないで帰ってきたんだ。(TJ/M)

*Kinō sa, depāto ni itta n' da kedo sa, hoshii mono ga nakute sa, kekkyoku nani mo kawanai de kaette kita n' da.*

So I go shopping yesterday, right, but there's really nothing there I want, so I just come home again without buying anything, you know?

A semantic breakdown of *sa*'s functions suggests four categories: (1) it emphasizes the correctness of a decisive statement or judgment you have just made; (2) it tells the other person to lighten up and not take things so seriously, or downplays the weight of what you just said or are about to say; (3) when used in combination with question words, it contributes to a sense of tension or confrontation; this sense of confrontation is heightened if the speaker is female; (4) in the forms *-te sa* or *to sa*, is used to report something you've heard.

(1) それは怒られてもしかたがないさ。君が悪いんだもの。(TJ/M)

*Sore wa okorarete mo shikata ga nai sa. Kimi ga warui n' da mono.*

So they got mad at you, what do you expect. After all, it was your fault.

批評するだけなら誰だってできるさ。(TJ/M)

*Hihyō suru dake nara dare datte dekiru sa.*

If all you're going to do is criticize, hey, anyone can do that.

(2) 別に深い意味はないんだ。ちょっと言ってみただけさ。(TJ/M)

*Betsu ni fukai imi wa nai n' da. Chotto itte mita dake sa.*

I didn't mean anything by it. I just felt like saying it.

まあいいさ。何とかなるよ。(TJ/M)

*Mā ii sa. Nan to ka naru yo.*

Well, not to worry. Things will work out one way or another.

(3) それならどうすればいいのさ。(TJ/M)

*Sore nara dō sureba ii no sa.*
Well, if that's the case, then what are we supposed do?

何さ、人が黙って聞いてりゃいい気になって。(TJ/F)
*Nani sa, hito ga damatte kiite rya ii ki ni natte.*
Listen, just because I'm not saying anything back doesn't mean you should get all smug and self-satisfied.
(*rya* is a tough-sounding abbreviation of *ireba*)

(4) 小林さん、転勤するんだって**さ**。(TJ/MF)
*Kobayashi-san, tenkin suru n' datte sa.*
They say that Kobayashi's about to get transferred.

けさ東北地方で地震があったんだ**とさ**。(TJ/M)
*Kesa Tōhoku chihō de jishin ga atta n' da to sa.*
They say there was an earthquake in Tōhoku this morning.

## • *Oi* as an "attention-getter" in male TJ

The interjection *oi* is used by men when calling out to their subordinates or close friends. When the would-be listener is at some distance, or for emphasis, the word may be repeated as in *oi oi* or lengthened to *ōi*.

おい、待てよ。そうあわてるな。(TJ/M)
*Oi, mate yo. Sō awateru na.*
Hey, slow down. What's the big rush?

おいおい、頼むよ。頼むから金を貸してくれ。(TJ/M)
*Oi oi, tanomu yo. Tanomu kara kane o kashite kure.*
Look! I'm asking you. Come on, loan me some money.

おおい、早く来いよ。こっちは見晴らしがいいぞ。(TJ/M)
*Ōi, hayaku koi yo. Kotchi wa miharashi ga ii zo.*
Hey! Come here, quick! The view from over here is terrific!

## • The many uses of *tte*

*Tte* can be called the colloquial equivalent of the classical expression *to te.* It has a casual sound and is more commonly used in T-Shirt than Necktie Japanese. It can be used in the following ways:

(1) When it precedes verbs like *iu* "say," *omou* "think" or *tanomu* "request," it outlines the substance of the statement,

thought or request. This same usage becomes *to* in more formal situations.

お医者さんに、当分アルコールは控えるようにって言われちゃったんだ。(TJ/M)

*Oisha-san ni, tōbun arukōru wa hikaeru yō ni **tte** iwarechatta n' da.*

The doctor told me to cut down on the drinking, for a while anyway.

あしたは友達と映画を見ようって約束したんです。(NJ/MF)

*Ashita wa tomodachi to eiga o miyō **tte** yakusoku shita n' desu.*

It's just that I made plans to go to the movies with a friend tomorrow.

(2) It can also signal that what follows is an explanation of what came just before. In more formal situations, or written Japanese, this is lengthened to *to iu (koto, mono, tokoro)*.

アメリカって国は広いね。(TJ/M)

*Amerika **tte** kuni wa hiroi ne.*

America's a pretty big country, isn't it?

今日は定休日だってこと、すっかり忘れていました。(NJ/MF)

*Kyō wa teikyū-bi da **tte** koto, sukkari wasurete imashita.*

I'd completely forgotten that today is the store's day off.

(3) *Tte* can also serve as a topic marker. In more formal speech, and in writing, this function is taken by *to iu no wa* or simply *wa*.

富士山って本当にきれいね。(TJ/F)

*Fujisan **tte** hontō ni kirei ne.*

Mt. Fuji sure is beautiful, isn't it?

黒沢さんって今どうしていらっしゃいますか? (NJ/MF)

*Kurosawa-san **tte** ima dō shite irasshaimasu ka?*

What has Kurosawa-san been doing recently?

(4) It can also be used to repeat some question, command or desire of the listener's as background for a comment that you wish to make. In more formal situations, this would be expressed as *to itte mo*.

今すぐ行けって、それは無理だよ。(TJ/M)
*Ima sugu ike tte, sore wa muri da yo.*
"Go now, immediately?" That's impossible.

誰がやったのかって、私に聞かれても知りませんよ。(NJ/MF)
*Dare ga yatta no ka tte, watashi ni kikarete mo shirimasen yo.*
You're asking me who did it? How should I know?

(5) At the end of sentences, *tte* can be used to indicate that the statement or claim is not your own ("they say," "I heard," etc.).

天気予報によると、午後から雨になるんだって。(TJ/MF)
*Tenki yohō ni yoru to, gogo kara ame ni naru n' datte.*
The weather forecast was saying it's going to rain this afternoon.

幸子さん、ひとり暮らしを始めたんですって。(NJ/F)
*Yukiko-san, hitori-gurashi o hajimeta n' desu tte.*
I hear Yukiko-san's moved out into her own place.

(6) *Tte* can also be used in questions that seek confirmation. In this usage, the intonation rises toward the end.

犯人が捕まったんだって。で、どういう人だったの。(TJ/MF)
*Hannin ga tsukamatta n' datte. De, dō iu hito datta no.*
So they caught the guy who did it, huh? What sort of person was he, anyhow?

「会社を辞める」ですって。いったいどうなさったんですか。
　(NJ/MF)
*"Kaisha o yameru" desu tte. Ittai dō nasatta n' desu ka.*
I hear you're going to quit. What in the world happened?

(7) Finally, *tte* can serve as a marker of reported speech, while implying skepticism, disbelief or scorn about the information conveyed.

「勉強しなさい」だって、もううんざりだよ。(TJ/M)
*"Benkyō shinasai" datte, mō unzari da yo.*
"Study, study, study!" Give me a break!

「私は何も知りません」ですって。(NJ/F)
*"Watashi wa nani mo shirimasen" desu tte.*
"I don't know anything about it." My foot!

# NECKTIE JAPANESE

André Bartsch works for Fuji Glass. During a lunchbreak, he talks with his boss, Takafumi Osawa.

**Ōsawa:** I tell you, my son's school had its parents and children's fitness day yesterday. I must have gone a little overboard, because I sure am feeling it today.

**Bartsch:** How old would your son be?

**Ōsawa:** He's in the fifth grade. I don't know which one of us he takes after, but he's full of the devil.

**Bartsch:** I see. And what contest did you enter?

**Ōsawa:** The bread-eating contest. My legs were killing me and I had started out the day with a hangover, too. It was awful, I tell you. And the wife was over on the sidelines yelling "Go for it!" at the top of her lungs and getting the whole thing on video, wouldn't you know it.

**Bartsch:** You know, Mr. Ōsawa, for a minute there I almost thought I detected a note of self-satisfaction in your voice. Well, at home, in any case, you're obviously a real go-getter.

**Ōsawa:** Now wait one minute. What is that supposed to mean, "at home"?

## ネクタイ

大沢　　いやあ、きのう子供の運動会ではりきっちゃったもんだから、あちこちが痛くて。参ったなあ。

バルシュ　**お子さんはおいくつなんですか。**

| 大沢 | 小学校5年生。誰に似たのか、こいつが腕白で腕白で。 |
|---|---|
| バルシュ | **それで、**どの競技に**出られたんですか。** |
| 大沢 | パン食い競争。足はつりそうになるわ、二日酔いだわでひどいめにあっちゃったよ。女房は「パパー!」なんて金切り声を張り上げながらビデオを回すしさ。 |
| バルシュ | でも、**課長、**満更でもなさそう**ですよ。ご家庭で**は大活躍**なんですね。** |
| 大沢 | おいおい、「ご家庭では」ってどういう意味だよ。 |

## NEKUTAI

**Ōsawa:** *Iyā, kinō kodomo no undō-kai de harikitchatta mon da kara, achi-kochi ga itakute. Maitta nā.*

**Barushu:** *Okosan wa oikutsu nan desu ka.*

**Ōsawa:** *Shōgakkō gonen-sei. Dare ni nita no ka, koitsu ga wanpaku de wanpaku de.*

**Barushu:** *Sore de, dono kyōgi ni derareta n' desu ka.*

**Ōsawa:** *Pankui kyōsō. Ashi wa tsurisō ni naru wa, futsuka-yoi da wa de hidoi me ni atchatta yo. Nyōbō wa "Papā!" nante kanakiri-goe o hariagenagara bideo o mawasu shi sa.*

**Barushu:** *Demo, kachō, manzara de mo nasasō desu yo. Gokatei de wa dai-katsuyaku nan desu ne.*

**Ōsawa:** *Oioi, "gokatei de wa" tte dō iu imi da yo.*

---

**NECKTIE NOTES**

• **Vertical relations in the workplace**

The basic unit of any organization in Japan is the hierarchical relationship, which can be based on age, seniority, duties and/or social status. Awareness of one's own relative position starts early: in Japanese schools, for example, students in the higher grades are referred to as the *senpai* ("seniors") of those who come after.

Language also clearly reflects each person's position in the social organization, requiring in many cases that people speak "up" or "down" to one another. So when Japanese meet people for the first time, they are likely to feel a bit uneasy and awkward until they determine their own relative position *vis-à-vis* the other.

This kind of hierarchical relationship tends to be fairly prominent and inflexible. It also follows the individuals wherever they go, inside or outside the workplace. If you call your boss *kachō* ("section chief") in a meeting, you also call him *kachō* on all other occasions. You do not ever "let down your hair" and call him by his first name over drinks or on the golf course. Furthermore, time and the tides of fortune have little effect on either one's overt role in a relationship or the language that corresponds to it. The aging, wealthy company executive will still call his high school teacher *sensei* and expect, in turn, to be called "~ *-kun.*"

## • *Kodomo-san, okosan, okosama*

In T-Shirt Japanese, one may refer to the children of one's friends and close acquaintances as *kodomo-san*, but in more formal language one should use a higher register: *okosan* or, to rise one step further, *okosama*. Such language reflects respect not for the child or children in question but rather for the relative status of their parents.

## • Honorific verb endings *-reru* and *-rareru*

*-Reru* and *-rareru* are primarily used to mark verbs in their passive, potential or spontaneous forms. They can also function, as in the dialogue, as honorific terms.

Whether a verb gets *-reru* or *-rareru* depends on what we might call the verb's "negative stem." Put the verb into the casual negative form: *ikanai, yomanai, tabenai,* etc. Then take off the *-nai.* If what you have left ends with "*a*," attach *-reru.* All other negative stems get *-rareru.*

| dictionary form | casual negative | negative stem | honorific |
|---|---|---|---|
| *iku* | *ikanai* | *ika* | *ikareru* |
| *yomu* | *yomanai* | *yoma* | *yomareru* |

| *taberu* | *tabenai* | *tabe* | *taberareru* |
|----------|-----------|--------|--------------|
| *miru*   | *minai*   | *mi*   | *mirareru*   |

The two exceptions are *suru* and *kuru*. These have irregular forms: *sareru* and *korareru*.

(1) (both NJ/MF; the first is a little more formal and respectful)

どちらまでいらっしゃいますか。　どちらまで**行かれ**ますか。

*Dochira made **irasshai**masu ka.　Dochira made **ikare**masu ka.*

How far are you going?

(2) (both NJ/MF; the first is a little more formal and respectful)

お昼は何**召し上がっ**たんですか。　お昼は何を**食べられ**たんですか。

*Ohiru wa nani o **meshiagat**ta n'　Ohiru wa nani o **taberare**ta desu ka.　n' desu ka.*

What did you have for lunch?

The *-reru* and *-rareru* forms are relatively low-level honorifics. So if there is a special honorific verb which can be substituted, it is more respectful (and so you might want to use it when you wish to express a fair amount of respect, for instance, to a former teacher). Thus, in a fairly formal situation, all the following alternatives for *kuru* ("come") are to be preferred to the simple *korareru*: *irassharu*, *oide ni naru*, *okoshi ni naru* and *omie ni naru*.

There is a tendency recently among young people to attach *-reru* to *all* negative stems, regardless of their conjugation. In other words, when forming the potential of certain verbs, they drop the "*-ra*" of "*-rareru*," turning, for instance, *mirareru* ("be able to see") into *mireru* and *taberareru* ("be able to eat") into *tabereru*, etc. This kind of usage often conveys an impression of slovenliness, as if the speaker were lisping. Students of the language are strongly urged not to follow native speakers in this practice, particularly in formal speech intended to convey respect.

## • What husbands and wives call one another

Until fairly recently, wives generally addressed their husbands with *anata* or by their personal names plus the deferential *-san*. For their part, husbands would call to their wives with the interjections *oi!* ("yo") or *chotto!* ("hey") and address them either with the somewhat rough, condescending *omae* or by their personal names without *-san*. But among younger people nowadays it is common for husbands to add *-san* to the wife's name. In some cases, couples drop *-san*, calling each other simply by their names or by some term of endearment.

Once they have children, couples sometimes call each other by the terms which their children use to address them: at first as *papa* and *mama*, and later as *otōsan* and *okāsan*. Some may use the still more formal variants *otōsama* and *okāsama*.

Many of the terms used to refer to one's own husband or wife hark back, at least superficially, to a time when men were the heads of households. So a woman will refer to her husband as *shujin* (lit. "master") while a man will usually call his wife *kanai* (lit. "[person] inside-the-house"). *Kanai* originally had a broader meaning, and could be used to refer to any member of a man's family, including the servants. It retains a humble nuance, and so can be used even in formal situations. You are likely to hear it used in phrases like *Yamashita no kanai de gozaimasu* ("[Takashi] Yamashita is my husband"/"I'm [Takashi] Yamashita's wife [~]") or *Kanai no Keiko de gozaimasu/desu*. This latter phrase can be spoken by the wife introducing herself ("I'm his wife Keiko") or by the husband to mean "This is my wife Keiko." But regardless of whether she or he says it, the inclusion of mention of a wife's first name in formal meetings is largely confined to younger people.

There are many other terms used to address or refer to spouses. *Otto* "my husband" and *tsuma* "my wife" are the most neutral of all, and both are frequently used not only in reference to a person's own spouse but also in a descriptive manner about "husbands" and "wives" in general, as in *otto to tsuma ga betsubetsu ni kurasu "tanshin-funin" ga ōku narimashita.* ("Cases of husbands and wives living separately because of a job transfer have grown more common").

There are several other popular words which mean "husband." These are *teishu* and *danna*, which reflect a time when the heads of households were also often merchants, innkeepers and tea shop proprietors. These words sound casual and are often used by local shopkeepers.

*Nyōbō* originally referred in the Heian period to ladies-in-waiting who served at court; in the modern language it has become a rather casual term for "wife." And as we saw in Chapter 2, *kami-san* is commonly used by merchants and artisans as a colloquial familiar term: *uchi no kami-san* "the Missus."

## • Calling fellow employees by their titles

As one might expect, given the hierarchical nature of Japanese society and the priority placed on social roles rather than individual personality, titles are often preferred over names at the workplace. In referring to the *kakari-chō* "chief clerk," *kachō* "section chief," *buchō* "division chief" or *shachō* "company president," one does not normally add the surname, unless some special or personal emphasis is called for, or there is potential for ambiguity.

In some companies, though, an effort is being made to "reform" this practice by encouraging the use of surname plus *-san* for all employees. Similar leveling is also evident in a growing tendency among academics, physicians and politicians to call one another simply *sensei* rather than more specific terms based on rank.

## • *Uchi* and *otaku*

*Katei* is a fairly narrow term, referring to your home or family (and *gokatei* is the counterpart which can be used for other people's). *Uchi* is broader because it can refer not only to your own house or household, but also to your business concern. The counterpart of *uchi*, used to refer to other people's companies, homes or families, is *otaku*.

> うちは女房と僕のふたりきりですが、**お宅**は何人家族ですか。
> (NJ/M)
>
> *Uchi wa nyōbō to boku no futari-kiri desu ga, **otaku** wa nan-nin kazoku desu ka.*
>
> It's just my wife and myself. How many are there in your family?

> うちは狭いし、マンションだからペットも飼えないの。**お宅**がうらやましいわ。(TJ/F)
>
> *Uchi wa semai shi, manshon da kara petto mo kaenai no. **Otaku** ga urayamashii wa.*
>
> Our place is really small, plus it's an apartment, so we're not allowed to have pets. You're lucky.

お宅のヒット商品には完全にやられましたよ。おかげで**うち**は最悪でした。(TJ/MF)

*Otaku no hitto shōhin ni wa kanzen ni yararemashita yo. Okage de **uchi** wa saiaku deshita.*

Your company's hit items have about done us in. Thanks to you, our business has really been on the skids!

## EQUIVALENCY CHART

| T-SHATSU | NEKUTAI |
|---|---|
| *kodomo-san* | *okosan* |
| *ikutsu* | *oikutsu* |
| *~ na no?* | *~ nan desu ka.* |
| *de,* | *sore de,* |
| *deta* | *derareta* |
| *~ no?* | *~ -n desu ka.* |
| *~ da yo.* (M) | *~ desu yo.* |
| *Ōsawa-san,* | *kachō,* |
| *uchi* | *gokatei* |
| *~ nan da ne.* (M) | *~ nan desu ne.* |

# My Lovely/Birdbrained Wife

愛妻は愚妻?

## T-SHIRT JAPANESE

In front of a supermarket late one Sunday afternoon, Fernando Ortega runs into his sandlot baseball buddy, Takashi Miura. Takashi is out shopping with his wife.

**Fernando:** Takashi, hi! Long time no see!

**Takashi:** Oh, hi. Sure has been a long time. So, what are you up to?

**Fernando:** Just going to do some shopping.

**Takashi:** (gesturing toward his wife) Hey, this is my wife.

**Mari:** Hello, nice to meet you. I've heard so much about you.

**Fernando:** Nice to meet you. Hey, Takashi, you didn't mention how lovely your wife was.

**Takashi:** Oh, now don't be saying anything like that, she'll get a swelled head! As it is now, she only brought me along today to have me carry the shopping bags for her.

**Fernando:** Speaking as a bachelor and all, I'd say you've got it pretty good. Well, see you around!

**Takashi:** Bye!

**Mari:** Nice to have met you!

# Tシャツ

| | |
|---|---|
| フェルナンド | **よう、三浦さん。しばらく。** |
| 孝 | あ、こんにちは。**しばらくだね。** きょうはど こへ? |
| フェルナンド | ちょっとそこまで**買い物に。** |
| 孝 | (奥さんを手で示しながら)オルテガさん、**これ、 うちの。** |
| 万里 | はじめまして。**いつも主人がお世話になりま して……。** |
| フェルナンド | **いいえ、こちらこそ。** 三浦さん、素敵な**奥さ んだね。** |
| 孝 | いやあ、**とんでもない。** 愚妻で……。きょう はせがまれて荷物持ちだよ。 |
| フェルナンド | 独身の僕にはそれもうらやましいな。**じゃあ また。** |
| 孝 | **じゃあ。** |
| 万里 | **どうも。** |

# T-SHATSU

| | |
|---|---|
| Ferunando: | *Yō, Miura-san.* **Shibaraku.** |
| Takashi: | *A, konnichiwa.* **Shibaraku da ne.** *Kyō wa* **doko e?** |
| Ferunando: | *Chotto soko made* **kaimono ni.** |
| Takashi: | *(Okusan o te de shimeshinagara) Orutega-san,* **kore, uchi no.** |
| Mari: | *Hajimemashite.* **Itsumo shujin ga osewa ni narimashite …** |
| Ferunando: | **Iie, kochira koso.** *Miura-san, suteki na* **okusan da ne.** |
| Takashi: | *Iyā,* **tonde mo nai.** *Gusai de … Kyō wa sega- marete nimotsu-mochi* **da yo.** |

**Ferunando:** *Dokushin no **boku** ni wa sore mo urayamashii na. Jā mata.*

**Takashi:** *Jā.*

**Mari:** *Dōmo.*

---

**T-SHIRT NOTES**

---

● *Yō* **as a male greeting**

*Yō* is commonly heard in conversation as a form of greeting called out from one man to another. It is more casual than *yā* and usually indicates a close sense of camaraderie. It also suggests mild surprise. A female equivalent is *ara*.

> よう、元気でやってる? (TJ/M)
> *Yō, genki de yatte 'ru?*
> Hi there, how's it going?

> よう、驚いたなあ。こんな所でばったり会うなんて。 (TJ/M)
> *Yō, odoroita nā. Konna tokoro de battari au nante.*
> Boy, what a surprise! Imagine running into you here!

> あら、青木さん、何年ぶりかしら。 (TJ/F)
> *Ara, Aoki-san, nan-nen-buri kashira.*
> Aoki-san, I can't believe it! How many years has it been?

> あら、すっかりスマートになられたので、見違えちゃったわ。 (TJ/F)
> *Ara, sukkari sumāto ni narareta no de, mi-chigaechatta wa.*
> My word, you've slimmed down so much I hardly recognized you!

● *Shibaraku*: **long time no see**

The adverb *shibaraku* literally means "for a while." The actual time elapsed can vary greatly, since the focus is on the speaker's subjective perception rather than on the actual length of time. Depending on the context, *shibaraku* can refer to a period in the past or future, either emphasizing or downplaying the length of time.

*Shibaraku* is generally used in three ways: (1) to refer to a period which may not be especially long but will be too long to be ignored ("just a minute"); (2) to describe noticeably longer time frames in the past ("a while," "some time"); and (3) to suggest actions that the listener might take for the time being.

(1) **しばらく**お待ちください。(NJ/MF)
*Shibaraku omachi kudasai.*
One moment, please.

悪いけど**しばらく**席をはずしてもらえないか。(TJ/M)
*Warui kedo shibaraku seki o hazushite moraenai ka.*
Sorry to bother you, but could you let us have the room for a minute (leave us alone for a minute)?

(2) こんなに雨が降るのは**しばらく**ぶりね。(TJ/F)
*Konna ni ame ga furu no wa shibaraku-buri ne.*
It's been quite a while since we've had a rain like this, hasn't it!

**しばらく**お見かけしませんでしたが、どこかへいらしていたんですか。(NJ/MF)
*Shibaraku omikake shimasen deshita ga, doko ka e irashite ita n' desu ka.*
I haven't seen you in a long time. Have you been away somewhere?

(3) 頭が痛いんなら、**しばらく**横になって様子を見たらどうだ? (TJ/M)
*Atama ga itai n' nara, shibaraku yoko ni natte yōsu o mitara dō da?*
If you have a headache, why not lie down for a few minutes and see if you feel any better?

コストの問題は**しばらく**置くとして、企画内容についてはどうでしょう。(NJ/MF)
*Kosuto no mondai wa shibaraku oku to shite, kikaku naiyō ni tsuite wa dō deshō.*
If we set aside the question of cost for the time being, what do you think about the content of the plan itself?

The second meaning is often used to refer to meetings with people after a long time has gone by. With friends or close acquaintances, simply saying *shibaraku* is enough. More formal situations calls for *shibaraku desu (ne)*. A synonym is *hisashi-buri*, though this tends to suggest a longer span of time than does *shibaraku*. In more polite—or typically feminine—speech, the honorific *o-* prefix is attached to this variant. Its alternatives, in ascending order of politeness, include *ohisashiburi*, *ohisashi-buri desu* and *ohisashiburi de gozaimasu*.

## • *A, a' and ā*

(1) The interjection *a*, like its variants *a'* (clipped) and *ā* (drawn out), expresses surprise or signals a thought suddenly recalled. (2) *A* and one of the variants, the lengthened *ā*, may also be used to attract someone's attention.

(1) あ、しまった。お財布を忘れちゃった。(TJ/MF)
   *A, shimatta. Osaifu o wasurechatta.*
   Oh, rats! I forgot my wallet (purse).

   (After stepping on someone's foot)
   あ、ごめんなさい。大丈夫ですか。(NJ/MF)
   *A, gomen nasai. Daijōbu desu ka.*
   Oops, sorry! Are you okay?

   あっ、大変だ。急がなくっちゃ。(TJ/MF)
   *A', taihen da. Isoganakutcha.*
   Oh, no! I've got to hurry!

(2) あ、君、悪いけど、コピーとってきてくれないか。(TJ/M)
   *A, kimi, warui kedo, kopii totte kite kurenai ka.*
   Oh sorry, but could you make some copies for me?

   あ、すみません。お水いただけますか。(NJ/MF)
   *A, sumimasen. Omizu itadakemasu ka.*
   Excuse me. Could I have some water?

   ああ、ちょっと。お客さん、定期券を見せてください。
      (NJ/MF)
   *Ā, chotto. Okyaku-san, teiki-ken o misete kudasai.*
   Uh, sir (ma'am, miss). Could I see your train pass, please?

## • *Kyō wa doko e* is not really a question

In more or less the same way that "How are you?" is a standard greeting that doesn't require a detailed response, Japanese use *kyō wa doko e* ("Where are you off to today?") with no intention of violating the other person's privacy. This phrase, like its variant *kyō wa doko made*, is simply meant to express general interest and goodwill.

## • *Chotto soko made* the properly vague response

When replying to the formulaic use of *kyō wa doko e*, it wouldn't be appropriate to outline the details of your schedule. You can say simply *chotto Shinjuku made* "I'm on my way to Shinjuku," *chotto kaimono ni* "I'm off to do a little shopping" or even *chotto soko made* "I'm just going out for a bit."

Other lightweight phrases that come in handy when you run into an acquaintance on the street include, of course, observations about the weather: *kyō mo atsui desu ne* "Hot enough for you?"; *yoku furimasu ne* "Sure is coming down, huh?"; and *hiemasu ne* "Chilly, isn't it?"

## • *Kore* to refer to your family, *are* for others

*Kore* ("this") usually refers to objects relatively close at hand, as seen from the speaker's point of view. But it can also be used to refer to family members. This usage dates back to classical Japanese of the Heian period; at that time people who were physically close by could be referred to as *kore*, and then the term conveyed a sense of respect. In the modern language, *kore* is a humble form used only to refer to one's own family members.

*Are* ("that [over there]") can also function as a personal pronoun. You use it when the person you are talking about is your social equal or ranked below you. It suggests a feeling of intimacy with the person being discussed.

(Usually referring to a male family member or a pet)
これがいたずらで、家中手を焼いているんだよ。(TJ/M)
*Kore ga itazura de, iejū te o yaite iru n' da yo.*
This guy keeps us all in an uproar with his shenanigans.

(Generally referring to a wife or child)
これが大変お世話になりまして、ありがとうございました。
  (NJ/MF)
*Kore ga taihen osewa ni narimashite, arigatō gozaimashita.*
She really appreciates all you've done for her.

あれには苦労ばかりかけて申し訳ないと思っているよ。
(TJ/M)
*Are ni wa kurō bakari kakete mōshi-wake nai to omotte iru yo.*
I know I haven't been a very good husband (father, etc.).

あれは出世しますよ。人の嫌がる仕事を苦にもしていません
からね。(NJ/M)
*Are wa shusse shimasu yo. Hito no iyagaru shigoto o ku ni mo shite imasen kara ne.*
That one's going to go far. She's happy to do the sort of work that other people complain about.

### • *Uchi no* to indicate one's wife or husband

In casual conversations with friends, people sometimes refer to their own husband or wife as *uchi no*. Wives often refer to their husbands as *uchi no hito* (lit., "the person of the house"). Husbands, in turn, often use *uchi no yatsu* (the literal translation is the same, but the nuance is rough or slightly derogatory).

うちのは甘いものが好きでね、四六時中食べてるよ。(TJ/M)
*Uchi no wa amai mono ga suki de ne, shirokuji-chū tabete 'ru yo.*
My wife loves sweets. She eats them round the clock.

うちのは毎晩帰りが遅いから、夕食いつもひとりなのよ。
(TJ/F)
*Uchi no wa maiban kaeri ga osoi kara, yūshoku itsumo hitori na no yo.*
My husband gets home late every night, so I always have supper alone.

### • *Hajimemashite*: Nice to meet you

*Hajimemashite* is a greeting exchanged by people meeting for the first time. When someone says *hajimemashite* to you, it is proper to repeat the same phrase back. You can add *yoroshiku onegai shimasu/itashimasu* after this phrase, if you like.

### • Trailing off before *arigatō*

When, in the TJ dialogue, Mr. Miura's wife says *"itsumo shujin ga osewa ni narimashite …,"* the implied conclusion to the sentence is *arigatō gozaimasu* "Thank you (for everything you have done for my husband)." While in formal speech it is not a good idea to economize in this way, it is common in everyday conversation to end formulaic thanks or apologies with *-te:* "*sukkari gochisō ni natte shimaimashite …*" (with the implied conclusion being *sumimasen/mōshi-wake gozaimasen deshita* or *arigatō gozaimashita*) "You've treated me to such a terrific meal (I'm very grateful/so embarrassed)." Other apologetic expressions include "*gomeiwaku o okake shimashite …*" "(I'm sorry for) all the inconvenience I've caused," *sukkari ojama shite shimaimashite …*" "(I'm sorry for) staying so long," and "*otesū o okake shimashite …*" "(I'm sorry for) putting you to all this trouble."

• *Kochira koso*

This common expression is used as a polite reciprocal response to statements directed to oneself, notably thanks or apologies. It may be compared to the set English expression "Likewise, I'm sure."

• *Gusai*: "My silly wife" suggests an easy intimacy

The word *gusai* (literally "my foolish wife") is simply another example of a polite, humble form. Generally used only in formal situations and often by older men, it has a kind of "homey" ring to it. Despite its literal meaning, it gives an impression of an easy camaraderie between husband and wife, and thus can be compared to such English phrases as "the wife" or "the Missus."

In Japan, disparaging one's in-group is an expression of modesty on the speaker's part. A man who refers to his wife as *gusai* doesn't mean to exalt himself at her expense. Older gentlemen also sometimes use *gusoku* to refer to a son, or *gukei* (*gumai*) about an older brother (younger sister). The prefix *gu-* means "silly," "foolish," "dull."

Another humble prefix is *setsu-* "clumsy, bungling." To refer to your own house, a book you wrote or your own artwork, you can say *settaku*, *setcho* and *sessaku* (the two latter appearing mostly in written form). It's also possible to speak, in casual conversation, of *abaraya* "my ramshackle home" or *uchi no doramusuko* "my ne'er-do-well son."

## • *Jā mata*: catch you later

*Ja* (or *jā*) is a short, casual word of farewell. It is a contraction of *de wa* "well, then." (The original meaning of *sayōnara*, by the way, is very similar. It derives from *sayō nara*, meaning *sō nara* "if it is to be so, then."

Variations on *ja* include *jā ne* "bye," *jā mata* "well, see you again" and *jā ato de* "see you later."

*Mata* "(see you) again" is another handy term. It can be used alone or with a word specifying the time: *mata ato de* "see you later," *mata ashita* "see you tomorrow" and *mata raishū* "until next week," etc.

In the TJ dialogue, Mari Miura uses *dōmo* when saying goodbye to Fernando. (For more information on *dōmo*, see Chapter 3, "Tied Up in a Meeting," page 53.)

# NECKTIE JAPANESE

In front of a department store late one Sunday afternoon, Fernando Ortega runs into Takashi Miura, a business associate. Mr. Miura is out shopping with his wife.

| | |
|---|---|
| **Ortega:** | Mr. Miura, hello there. I haven't seen you in a while. |
| **Miura:** | Oh, hello. It has been a long time, hasn't it? So what brings you out here today? |
| **Ortega:** | Just out doing an errand or two. |
| **Miura:** | (gesturing toward his wife) Mr. Ortega, I'd like you to meet my wife. |
| **Mrs. Miura:** | How do you do? I'm very pleased to meet you. |
| **Ortega:** | It's my pleasure. What a lovely wife you have, Mr. Miura! |
| **Miura:** | You think so? I tend to forget now and then. Today, for instance, she only brought me along to act as the porter! |
| **Ortega:** | Speaking as a bachelor, I'm green with envy. Well, I had best be on my way. |
| **Miura:** | Good-bye. |
| **Mrs. Miura:** | Good-bye. |

## ネクタイ

| | |
|---|---|
| オルテガ | 三浦さん、こんにちは。ご無沙汰しております。 |
| 三浦 | あ、こんにちは。こちらこそご無沙汰しております。きょうはどちらへ。 |
| オルテガ | 用事がありまして、ちょっとそこまで。 |

三浦 　　　(奥さんを手で示しながら)オルテガさん、**家内です。**

三浦夫人 　はじめまして。**いつも主人がお世話になっており
　　　　　ます。**

オルテガ 　**いいえ、こちらこそご主人様にお世話になりまし
　　　　　て……。**三浦さん、素敵な**奥様**ですね。

三浦 　　　いやあ、**とんでもありません。**愚妻でして……。
　　　　　きょうはせがまれまして荷物持ちですよ。

オルテガ 　独身の私にはそれもうらやましいですね。それで
　　　　　はまた。**失礼します。**

三浦 　　　**失礼します。**

三浦夫人 　**ごめんください。**

# NEKUTAI

| | |
|---|---|
| **Orutega:** | *Miura-san, konnichiwa. Gobusata shite ori-masu.* |
| **Miura:** | *A, konnichi wa.* **Kochira koso gobusata shite orimasu.** *Kyō wa* **dochira e.** |
| **Orutega:** | *Yōji ga arimashite,* chotto soko made. |
| **Miura:** | (Okusan o te de shimeshinagara) Orutega-san, **kanai desu.** |
| **Miura fujin:** | *Hajimemashite.* **Itsumo shujin ga osewa ni natte orimasu.** |
| **Orutega:** | **Iie, kochira koso goshujin-sama ni osewa ni narimashite …** Miura-san, suteki na **okusama desu ne.** |
| **Miura:** | *Iyā,* **tonde mo arimasen.** Gusai deshite … Kyō wa segamare**mashite,** nimotsu-mochi **desu yo.** |
| **Orutega:** | Dokushin no **watashi** ni wa sore mo uraya-mashii **desu ne.** Sore de wa mata. **Shitsurei shimasu.** |
| **Miura:** | **Shitsurei shimasu.** |
| **Miura fujin:** | **Gomen kudasai.** |

## • *Gobusata*

This is a fixed humble expression used to "chastise" yourself for having gotten out of touch, when you see or speak with an acquaintance again after some time has gone by.

*Gobusata* is followed by various forms of *suru* or *itasu* "do": *gobusata shite imasu, gobusata shite orimasu, gobusata itashite orimasu, gobusata shimashita, gobusata itashimashita.*

The implications of *gobusata* are apologetic: "I haven't been good about staying in touch with you." As with many other such polite phrases, it can be used in a *pro forma* way when, in fact, no one is really to blame. The phrase can be used toward people ranked higher than, lower than and the same as you, though the general rule is for the "junior member" in the relationship to take the initiative.

## • *Other polite inquiries*

After apologizing for the gap in communication, you should probably make some polite inquiries. These can include *ogenki de irasshaimasu ka* "How are you" *ikaga osugoshi desu ka* "How are things with you" and *okawari arimasen ka* (lit., "Are there not any changes") "Are you keeping well?" You can also ask about a person's work or family: *oshigoto no hō wa ikaga desu ka* "How's the job going" or *gokazoku no katagata wa ogenki de irasshaimasu ka* "How is your family."

*Kyō wa dochira e*, in sharp contrast to the direct English translation "Where are you going today," falls into this category of *pro forma* solicitude.

You can also resort to compliments, for instance: *ogenki-sō desu ne* "you look well," *aikawarazu gokatsuyaku de* "You seem to be (keeping) as active (busy) as ever" or *zenzen okawari ni narimasen ne* "You haven't changed a bit!"

## • Polite terms for other people's spouses

In formal situations, people generally refer to others' wives as *okusama* and others' husbands as *goshujin-sama*. The more relaxed contractions of these terms are *okusan* and *goshujin*.

In earlier ages, *okusama* was used to refer to the main wives of aristocrats and feudal lords. This usage then spread to the higher-ranking social strata of warriors and wealthy merchants. The term used by most ordinary townspeople during the Edo period was *okami-san*, which was a polite term. *Okami-san* is still used today, particularly by merchants and traditional craftsmen. The casual contraction is *kami-san*. (-*San* has become a permanent part of the word, which makes *kami-san* an exception to the rule that prohibits attaching -*san* to any term you use to talk about your in-group to outsiders).

Alternative terms for other people's husbands are *danna-sama*, *danna-san* and *goteishu*. Despite the honorific prefix attached to this last, the term does not convey a strong sense of respect and therefore should not be used in reference to the husbands of one's social betters. *Danna* comes originally from the Sanskrit *dāna pati* (lit. "alms master") and was used by Buddhist temple monks in polite reference to those who made offerings. By extension, *danna* took on the general meaning of "master." It was used as a term of address for shopkeepers and others. In older times, some women of the warrior and merchant classes called their husbands *danna-sama* when addressing them directly, but this usage has almost entirely disappeared. In the small number of Japanese households that still employ them, maids use *danna-sama* when addressing the man of the house.

### • *Iyā tonde mo arimasen*: denigrating your in-group

In Japanese, saying "thank you" in response to a compliment would suggest that you accept and agree with the words of praise and would sound self-centered. The polite course is always to demur, as Takashi Miura does in response to Fernando Ortega's praise of his wife. The word *iyā* is a T-shirt, male variation of *iie*. It appears here in both dialogues, adding a lighthearted touch to Mr. Miura's statement about his wife.

When deflecting words of admiration for specific abilities or accomplishments, you can say: *iie, magure desu* "Oh, it was just a fluke" or *iie, taishita koto de wa nai n' desu* "It's really nothing."

Another strategy for conveying a sense of modesty is pointing out that one's success is dependent on others: *kore mo hitoe ni mina-sama no okage desu* "This too is completely due to your help." If a colleague, for instance, or anyone other than a very close friend should compliment you on your handsome watch, it's probably best to respond, *demo, kore yasu-mono na no yo* "Oh, but it's quite inexpensive."

Nowadays, with Western influence, especially from America, some young people react to compliments with a frank, affirmative *arigatō*.

### • Saying good-bye in NJ

Different phrases are used in various situations as Necktie farewells. Both *shitsurei shimasu/itashimasu* and *gomen kudasai* are quite commonly used in many different contexts. These two phrases are equally appropriate when you leave a company after visiting there on business, or when you take your leave from a party at someone's house. Should you expect to see the person again soon, you might want to say *mata nochi-hodo* "See you soon" or, a little less specifically, *sore de wa mata* "See you again." Either of these two expressions can be followed up, for greater formality, with *ome ni kakarimasu* "I will see you" or *oaishimasu* "We will meet," both of which are honorific. If you are to see the person the following day, you can say *mata myōnichi [raishū] ome ni kakarimasu* "So then, we'll meet again tomorrow (next week)."

## EQUIVALENCY CHART

| T-SHIRT JAPANESE | NECKTIE JAPANESE |
|---|---|
| *Yō, Miura-san.* | *Miura-san, konnichiwa.* |
| *Shibaraku.* | *Gobusata shite orimasu.* |
| *Shibaraku da ne.* | *Kochira koso gobusata shite orimasu.* |
| *doko e?* | *dochira e?* |
| *kaimono ni.* | *Yōji ga arimashite,* |
| *kore, uchi no.* | *kanai desu.* |

*Itsumo shujin ga
   osewa ni narimashite ...*
*Iie, kochira koso.*

*okusan*
*~ da ne.* (M)
*tonde mo nai.*
*~ de ...*
*~ -te*
*~ da yo.* (M)
*boku* (M)
*~ na.*
*Jā mata.*

*Jā.*
*Dōmo.*

*Itsumo shujin ga osewa ni
   natte orimasu.*
*Iie, kochira koso goshujin-
   sama ni osewa ni narimashite ...*
*okusama*
*~ desu ne.*
*tonde mo arimasen.*
*~ deshite ...*
*~ -mashite*
*~ desu yo.*
*watashi*
*~ desu ne.*
*Sore de wa mata. Shitsurei
   shimasu.*
*Shitsurei shimasu.*
*Gomen kudasai.*

# Straight Talk

## 禅問答?

## T-SHIRT JAPANESE

Jagdeep Singh Sahni works for Indo-Japan Trading. He and colleague Hiroshi Watanabe made an appointment a few days ago to play golf with a client, but Hiroshi has just realized that the date conflicts with his department's redesign of the office layout. Hiroshi leans toward canceling the appointment right away.

| | |
|---|---|
| **Hiroshi:** | Hey, about that golf thing. I wonder. What do you think? |
| **Jagdeep:** | What do you mean? |
| **Hiroshi:** | I'm not sure we can pull it off. |
| **Jagdeep:** | Yeah, maybe you're right. |
| **Hiroshi:** | Maybe we ought to just take a rain check this time. |
| **Jagdeep:** | Umm. |
| **Hiroshi:** | Wouldn't that be just as well for the client, too? |
| **Jagdeep:** | Maybe so. Well, maybe that's the way to go, then. |

## Tシャツ

| | |
|---|---|
| 宏 | こないだのゴルフの件だけどね。どうかな、あれは。 |
| ジャグディープ | ……と言うと? |
| 宏 | 無理だと思うよ。 |
| ジャグディープ | そうかな。 |

134

| 宏 | この際断った方がいいだろ。 |
| ジャグディープ | そうかもな。 |
| 宏 | 向こうもかえってその方がいいんじゃないかな。 |
| ジャグディープ | まあね。じゃあそうするか。 |

# T-SHATSU

| Hiroshi: | *Konaida no gorufu no ken da kedo ne. Dō ka na, are wa.* |
| Jagudiipu: | *... to iu to?* |
| Hiroshi: | *Muri da to omou yo.* |
| Jagudiipu: | *Sō ka na.* |
| Hiroshi: | *Kono sai kotowatta hō ga ii daro.* |
| Jagudiipu: | *Sō ka mo na.* |
| Hiroshi: | *Mukō mo kaette sono hō ga ii n' ja nai ka na.* |
| Jagudiipu: | *Mā ne. Jā sō suru ka.* |

---

### T-SHIRT NOTES

• *Konaida*: a contraction of *kono aida*

*Kono aida* (lit., "this interval") refers to a relatively recent point in the past and is therefore comparable to English "the other day." In conversation, it is commonly contracted to *konaida*.

> こないだ借りたお金、返すわ。ありがとう。(TJ/F)
> *Konaida karita okane, kaesu wa. Arigatō.*
> Here's the money you lent me the other day. Thanks.

> こないだ東京駅でばったり高校時代の同級生に会いましてね、驚きました。(NJ/MF)
> *Konaida Tōkyō eki de battari kōkō-jidai no dōkyū-sei ni aimashite ne, odorokimashita.*
> The other day I ran into an old high-school classmate in Tokyo Station—boy, was I surprised!

• *No ken:* **the matter of**

*Ken* is used (1) as an independent noun meaning "matter," "affair," "case," "subject," and (2) as a counter for cases or instances.

In the first usage, it normally follows a modifying phrase or clause, as in ~ *no ken*, ~ *shita ken*, etc. It's often used when two people are returning to a topic they have discussed before ("about that ~ ").

(1) きのう相談した**件**だけどね、あれ、どうする？ (TJ/MF)
*Kinō sōdan shita **ken** da kedo ne, are, dō suru?*
That matter we talked over yesterday, what do you want to do about it?

ゆうべの**件**ですが、その後、進展はありましたか。 (NJ/MF)
*Yūbe no **ken** desu ga, sono go, shinten wa arimashita ka.*
On that subject we discussed last night, has there been any progress?

(2) ここ5、6**件**同じような事件が続いているけど、同一人物の犯行かしら。 (TJ/F)
*Koko go, rok**ken** onaji yō na jiken ga tsuzuite iru kedo, dōitsu jinbutsu no hankō kashira.*
This is the fifth or sixth case of this sort in a row that we've seen recently. Could the same person be behind them all?

この商品については、驚いたことに1日に10**件**以上の問い合わせがあります。 (NJ/MF)
*Kono shōhin ni tsuite wa, odoroita koto ni ichinichi ni juk**ken** ijō no toiawase ga arimasu.*
I was surprised to see that there have been at least ten inquiries about this item every day.

• **Introducing topics with** *da kedo* **and** *desu ga*

Conjunctions *kedo* and *ga* may look at first glance as if they would mark an adversarial contrast between two statements, serving to deny or contradict what came before. But particularly when used after a noun, in phrases such as ~ *da kedo* they serve instead as links, functioning to introduce a topic. In Necktie conversation, these become ~ *desu ga* or ~ *de gozaimasu ga*.

こないだの話**だけど**、チャンスだからやっぱりやってみようと思うの。 (TJ/F)

*Konaida no hanashi **da kedo**, chansu da kara yappari yatte miyō to omou no.*

About what we were talking about the other day ... I think it's a good opportunity and I definitely want to give it a try.

(Spoken by a teacher to a student's parents)

お子さんの進学問題ですが、ご両親はどういうお考えですか。
(NJ/MF)

*Okosan no shingaku mondai **desu ga**, goryōshin wa dō iu okangae desu ka.*

What do you have in mind for the next stage of her education (what school would you like to see her enter)?

● *Dō ka na, are wa ...*

Technically, Japanese sentences are to end with a verb, *desu* or a sentence-final particle (*ne, yo*, etc.). However in practice, and especially in the spoken language, certain words and phrases are sometimes given additional emphasis by restructuring a sentence so that they come first. In Japanese grammar, this phenomenon is known as *tōchi-hō*, or inversion. With inversion, some of the main phrases are thrown in as an afterthought, which serves to highlight what has been pushed forward in the word order.

うまいんだなあ、これが。(TJ/M)
*Umai n' da nā, kore ga.* (Usually, *Kore ga umai n' da nā.*)
Good stuff, this!

ちょっと取ってくれる、それ。(TJ/MF)
*Chotto totte kureru, sore.* (Usually, *Chotto sore totte kureru.*)
That one there, could you get it for me.

いやになっちゃうわ、もう。(TJ/F)
*Iya ni natchau wa, mō.* (Usually, *Mō iya ni natchau wa.*)
I'm getting sick of it, really!

● *"... To iu to?"* an easy way to get more information

*"... To iu to"* ("which means "so you mean to say ...?"") is used to prompt a conversational partner to explain a statement more clearly or fully.

## • An implicit comfort

When speaking with intimates and others with whom there is a solid basis for understanding, Japanese often do not feel any need or desire to fill in all the fine details, preferring the implicit to the explicit. Looking at the dialogue above, for example, we see that Hiroshi starts off with *konaida no gorufu no ken* and then, when Jagdeep has responded, continues with *muri da to omou yo*. He assumes that Jagdeep will understand that the upcoming departmental business is the reason that the golf outing will not work out. When he says *kono sai kotowatta hō ga ii daro*, the implication is that they should not put matters off. The same idea is suggested in *mukō mo kaette sono hō ga ii n' ja nai ka:* i.e., the sooner they let their client know, the better.

In Japan, pleasant conversation consists largely of surmising what the other person thinks and dovetailing the flow of your own thoughts more closely to that of the other's. It's also important once in a while to anticipate your conversational partner's next move while you go about making your own. Focusing only on surface meaning and neglecting the deeper background is a formula for misunderstandings and frustration.

## • At this juncture: *kono sai*

*Sai* means "occasion," "time" or "case." The set phrase *kono sai* has the rather dramatic nuance of "at this (critical) juncture." It often refers to a point in time at which some action—whether large or small—is taken. The expression basically has the same meaning as *kono bāi* "in this case," or *kono toki* "on this occasion," but is richer with implication.

## • *Darō* and *deshō*

*Darō* combines the auxiliary verbs *da* and *u*. The former has the function of making sentences into declarative statements, while the latter adds a sense of conjecture. Both *darō* and its more casual, abrupt-sounding form *daro* are used by men in casual conversation. Women use *deshō* and *desho*, both of which derive from the auxiliary verb *desu*. *Darō* and *deshō* can be preceded by verbs in the dictionary form (such as *iku* "go" or *yameru* "quit") or by nouns, adjectives or adverbs. In general, *darō* can be shortened to *daro* only when it appears at the ends of sentences.

*Darō* and *deshō* have five main uses:

(1) The first of these is to outline some supposition or imagining of the speaker's which is rooted in fact.

多分あしたは晴れる**だろ**。(TJ/M)
*Tabun ashita wa hareru **daro**.*
Tomorrow the weather will probably clear up.

今頃みんなで楽しくやっているん**だろう**な。(TJ/M)
*Imagoro minna de tanoshiku yatte iru n' **darō** na.*
I bet they're all having a grand old time about now.

(2) The terms can also be used to pose an actual or a rhetorical question, with or without *ka*.

お父さん、何時頃帰ってくるん**だろう**。(TJ/M)
*Otōsan, nanji goro kaette kuru n' **darō**.*
I wonder what time Father will get home.

そんなうまい話ってある**だろう**か。(TJ/M)
*Sonna umai hanashi tte aru **darō** ka.*
That sounds too good to be true. (lit., "Could there be such a sweet story [deal]?")

(3) *Darō* and *deshō* also describe hypothetical situations. In this usage, *darō* is optional and is often dropped.

オーストラリアへ行ったら、楽しく暮らせる（**だろう**）と思うけどね。(TJ/M)
*Ōsutoraria e ittara, tanoshiku kuraseru (**darō**) to omou kedo ne.*
I really do think we could have a nice life if we went to Australia.

彼女は努力家だから、何をしても成功する（**だろう**）ことは間違いないよ。(TJ/M)
*Kanojo wa doryoku ka da kara, nani o shite mo seikō suru (**darō**) koto wa machigainai yo.*
She's a hard worker, so I'm sure she will succeed at anything she sets out to do.

(4) They can also be used in the construction *darō ni* to describe an imagined case which is contrary to fact.

もう少し早く起きていたら、こんなにあわてなくてすんだ**だ
ろうに**。(TJ/MF)

*Mō sukoshi hayaku okite itara, konna ni awatenakute sunda
**darō** ni.*

If I had only gotten up a little earlier, I wouldn't have had to
rush around like this.

電車が1本違っていたら、会うことはなかった**だろうに**、本
当に偶然だね。(TJ/M)

*Densha ga ippon chigatte itara, au koto wa nakatta **darō** ni,
hontō ni gūzen da ne.*

If I had caught any other train, we'd probably never have met!
It's quite a coincidence!

(5) Finally, they are useful in seeking the listener's agreement. In
this case, *darō* or *deshō* is spoken with a rising intonation.

今更そんなこと言われたって困る**だろ**。(TJ/M)

*Imasara sonna koto iwareta tte komaru **daro**.*

Isn't it a little late for me to be hearing this now?

君も聞いた**だろう**、あの話。(TJ/M)

*Kimi mo kiita **darō**, ano hanashi.*

I'm sure you heard it too, that story.

### • *Kamo* and *kamo shirenai*

These common expressions indicate that something is possible or
thinkable, though it may or may not be the case. They are similar
to the English "could be," "must be," "might be." The T-Shirt
*kamo shirenai* can be abbreviated to *kamo*, which sounds lighter.
It can be combined with sentence-final particles to make *kamo ne*,
*kamo na* and *kamo yo*. The NJ equivalent is *kamo shiremasen*.

今頃、日光は紅葉がきれい**かもしれない**な。(TJ/M)

*Imagoro, Nikkō wa kōyō ga kirei **kamo shirenai** na.*

Ah, the autumn leaves in Nikko must be pretty about now.

きょうはひょっとすると雨が降る**かもしれない**ね。(TJ/MF)

*Kyō wa hyotto suru to ame ga furu **kamo shirenai** ne.*

It could just rain today, you know.

**かもね**。(TJ/MF)

***Kamo** ne.*

It could.

こんな日は熱燗で鍋っていうのはどう？ (TJ/MF)
*Konna hi wa atsukan de nabe tte iu no wa dō?*
On a (cold) day like this, how about a pot of something and
  some hot saké?

いいかもね。(TJ/MF)
*Ii kamo ne.*
Sounds like a good idea.

## • *Mukō* and *senpō*

You can use either of these terms to refer to "the other party" involved with you or your in-group in some kind of activity or
dealings. The more formal term, the Sino-Japanese *senpō*, is preferred in Necktie situations. Some people use *mukō* when referring to their spouse in conversation with close friends.

向こうの言い分も聞こうじゃないか。(TJ/M)
*Mukō no ii-bun mo kikō ja nai ka.*
Come on, let's listen to what they've got to say about it, too.

向こうは何を考えているんだか、さっぱりわからないわ。
  (TJ/F)
*Mukō wa nani o kangaete iru n' da ka, sappari wakaranai wa.*
I have no idea what he is (they are) thinking!

## • *Kaette*

*Kaette* is a very handy word meaning "contrary to expectation,"
"rather" or "strangely enough." *Kaette* describes two possible outcomes or courses of action and expresses the speaker's sense that
one or the other of the two is preferable because more desirable,
suitable, etc.

やせようと思ってダイエットしたのに、**かえって**太っちゃっ
  たわ。(TJ/F)
*Yaseyō to omotte daietto shita no ni, **kaette** futotchatta wa.*
I went on a diet to lose weight, but in fact I ended up gaining.

この時間は車をひろうより電車で行った方が**かえって**早いで
  しょう。(NJ/MF)
*Kono jikan wa kuruma o hirou yori densha de itta hō ga
  **kaette** hayai deshō.*

At this time of day it might be faster to go by train, rather than
try to get a cab.

## • Mā ne

A conveniently vague phrase, *mā ne* is very handy. It means
something like "hmm … well, I suppose." A masculine variant is
*mā na*.

いろいろ大変だったんだって? (TJ/MF)
*Iroiro taihen datta n' datte?*
I hear you had a dreadful time of it.
まあね。ちょっとね。(TJ/MF)
*Mā ne. Chotto ne.*
Um, yeah. I suppose you could say that.

元気? (TJ/MF)
*Genki?*
How you doing?
うん、まあね。(TJ/MF)
*Un, mā ne.*
So-so.

## • Nodding to yourself in agreement, with *ka*

*Ka* is usually used at the end of sentences and clauses to ask an
actual or a rhetorical question, or to refute, persuade or request.
*Ka* can also be used as a rhetorical device for exclaiming aloud
to yourself or for musing on something suddenly realized or recalled.

もうお昼か。早いなあ。(TJ/M)
*Mō ohiru ka. Hayai nā.*
Noon already? Time flies!

そうですか、男の子が生まれたんですか。(NJ/MF)
*Sō desu ka, otoko no ko ga umareta n' desu ka.*
Really! They (she) had a boy!

# NECKTIE JAPANESE

Jagdeep Singh Sahni works for Indo-Japan Trading. His department head, Hiroshi Watanabe, buttonholes him one day to talk about a deal that they have been trying to work out with Yamakawa Trading Company. Watanabe has pretty much decided that the deal doesn't look so promising after all, and that he'd like to back out.

**Watanabe:** You know about that proposed deal with Yama-kawa Trading Company? Well, we've been doing some thinking.

**Sahni:** And what were you thinking?

**Watanabe:** I just don't see how we're going to work out the problems involved in it.

**Sahni:** Yes, maybe you're right.

**Watanabe:** So, at this point, I think maybe we would do well to let them know as soon as possible.

**Sahni:** Maybe that's best.

**Watanabe:** I think Yamakawa would actually appreciate it.

**Sahni:** I see. Well then, I'll start moving on it right away.

## ネクタイ

渡辺　**例の山川物産の件なんだけどね。どうかねえ、あれは。**

サーニ　……とおっしゃいますと？

渡辺　**ちょっと難しいと思わないか。**

サーニ　そうでしょうか。

渡辺　この際はっきりさせておいた方がいいんじゃないか
　　　ね。

サーニ　そうかもしれませんね。

渡辺　先方もかえってその方が助かるんじゃないかと思う
　　　けどね。

サーニ　はあ。では早速その方向で検討いたします。

## NEKUTAI

| | |
|---|---|
| **Watanabe:** | *Rei no Yamakawa Bussan no ken **nan da kedo** **ne**. Dō ka nē, are wa.* |
| **Sāni:** | *… to osshaimasu to?* |
| **Watanabe:** | *Chotto muzukashii to omowanai ka.* |
| **Sāni:** | *Sō deshō ka.* |
| **Watanabe:** | *Kono sai **hakkiri sasete oita** hō ga ii n' ja nai ka ne.* |
| **Sāni:** | *Sō kamo shiremasen ne.* |
| **Watanabe:** | *Senpō mo kaette sono hō ga **tasukaru** n' ja nai ka to omou kedo ne.* |
| **Sāni:** | *Hā. **De wa sassoku sono hōkō de kentō itashimasu.*** |

---

### NECKTIE NOTES

---

● **Dropping honorifics when you're the boss**

The Japanese language reflects a society that is still overtly hierarchical. Thus, as we saw in Chapter 6, we are required to use formal, even honorific language when addressing our superiors but do not expect the same in return. Bosses are allowed—indeed often expected—to "talk down" to their subordinates. Company presidents may say to their secretaries: *Oi, kimi, kono kopii ichibu, isogi de ne* "Hey you, get me a copy of this, will you, on the double!"

Many non-Japanese may find this "bossy" attitude surprising

or even offensive and yet, personal feelings and judgments aside, this is a reality that it's best to come to terms with. On the other hand, it's impossible to make sweeping generalizations. There are many exceptions: some people, for reasons of principle or personality, or in keeping with the atmosphere of their organization, use more or less the same polite level of speech with everyone. It's best, too, not to jump to the naive conclusion that rough-sounding language implies ridicule or that polite forms necessarily indicate genuine respect, since ordinary psychological distance between speaker and listener also helps to dictate the level of politeness used.

In the dialogue, Mr. Watanabe, as the superior, chose to phrase many of his statements to Mr. Sahni quite casually. Had he preferred to, he could have said the same things a little more deferentially:

例の山川物産の件なんですけどね。
*Rei no Yamakawa Bussan no ken nan **desu** kedo ne.*

どうですかねえ、あれは。
*Dō **desu** ka nē, are wa.*

ちょっと難しいと思いませんか。
*Chotto muzukashii to **omoimasen ka**.*

この際はっきりさせておいた方がいいん（よろしい）んじゃないですかね。
*Kono sai hakkiri sasete oita hō ga ii (**yoroshii**) n' ja nai **desu** ka ne.*

先方もかえってその方が助かるんじゃないかと思いますけどね。
*Senpō mo kaette sono hō ga tasukaru n' ja nai ka to **omoimasu** kedo ne.*

## • *Rei no* as insider talk

*Rei* is an insider code. It means (1) a topic that the speaker and listener recently discussed or both know about. In other words, the phrase could be translated as "you know—that thing we talked about." *Rei no* is useful from the points of view of verbal economy and discretion. Anybody listening in on the conversation above would know that it concerns Yamakawa Trading Company, but would not have access to any further details.

*Rei* can also be used to mean (2) "the usual," referring to the same place, method or choice (of food or drink, etc.) as always.

(1) 例の人とはどうなった? (TJ/MF)
   *Rei no* hito to wa dō natta?
   How did it work out between you and her (that girl)?

   例の札幌行きの話ですが、やはりちょっと無理だと思うんです。 (NJ/MF)
   *Rei no* Sapporo-yuki no hanashi desu ga, yahari chotto muri da to omou n' desu.
   About that Sapporo trip we talked about, I just don't think it will work out.

(2) 何にしますか。 (NJ/MF)
   *Nani ni shimasu ka.*
   What would you like?
   例のやつをもらおうか。 (TJ/M)
   *Rei no* yatsu o moraō ka.
   Just give me the usual.

   例のとこ、きょうも行きませんか。 (NJ/MF)
   *Rei no* toko, kyō mo ikimasen ka.
   Shall we make it the usual place again today?

### • *Nan desu* for emphasis

The *nan da* seen in the dialogue is the contracted form of *na no da*. *Nan da* is often used in spoken Japanese. It is used to emphasize or underscore declarative statements.

In Necktie situations these phrases become the very proper *na no desu* and the slightly more conversational *nan desu*.

A side-by-side comparison of sentences with and without *nan desu* may be of some help.

| | |
|---|---|
| これこそ僕のやりたかった仕事だ。 | これこそ僕のやりたかった仕事なんだ。 |
| *Kore koso boku no yaritakatta shigoto da.* (TJ/M) | *Kore koso boku no yaritakatta shigoto nan da.* (TJ/M) |
| This is the work I wanted to do! | This is precisely the work I wanted to do! |

あしたから岩国へ出張です。　あしたから岩国へ出張**なんです**。
*Ashita kara Iwakuni e*　　　*Ashita kara Iwakuni e shutchō*
　*shutcho desu.* (NJ/MF)　　　**nan desu**. (NJ/MF)
I'm leaving for Iwakuni on　It's just that I'm leaving for
　business tomorrow.　　　　Iwakuni on business tomorrow.

● *"... To osshaimasu to?"*

*"... To osshaimasu to?"* is the Necktie counterpart of *"... to iu to?"* *Ossharu* is, as we have seen before, the honorific form of *iu* ("to say"). This phrase is a polite way to prompt your conversational partner to give more information: "So you mean to say ...?"

Foreign learners of Japanese should be careful not to imitate two phrases commonly used by native speakers which are actually grammatically incorrect. Instead of the honorific verb *ossharu*, native speakers sometimes use the humble verb *mōsu* by mistake. You will hear both *"... to mōshimasu to?"* and *"... to mōsaremasu to?"* The latter consists of *mōsu* with the honorific verb ending *-rareru* attached.

● **The gentle art of indirectness**

Understatement and other euphemistic expressions are extremely common in the speech of Japanese adults. They are not used to conceal the truth so much as to maintain psychological and social distance by steering clear of explicit statements. This kind of distance is to be desired when the listener is a superior, a relative stranger or anyone else with whom one does not wish to be "linguistically intimate." Experienced Japanese speakers know when they hear *chotto muzukashii* that this does not mean "a bit difficult" but "impossible" or "out of the question," although these blunter terms could easily be expressed with *muri da* "impossible," *fukanō da* "not possible" or *dame da* "no go." Likewise, the literal meaning of the *hakkiri sasete oita hō ga ii* of the dialogue is "it is better to make matters clear," but the sentence's implication is obviously, "We're going to have to say no."

In addition to this kind of obliqueness, one common euphemistic strategy is to substitute different words for troublesome terms, such as *nakunaru* "pass away" for *shinu* "die" or *akusei shuyō* "malignant tumor" instead of *gan* "cancer." Another is simply to pad the entire sentence with verbal softeners to make it sound more oblique.

In Japanese, people very often combine euphemistic remarks with polite softeners in order to adjust the tone of their sentences. As language learners become more adept at spotting the psychological or social distance hidden inside oblique statements, it becomes much easier to understand what people are trying to say.

Learning when to take a statement as sincere and when to interpret it as a polite cliché is essential. Taken literally and out of context, *kangaesasete itadakimasu* may seem to suggest "We shall take the matter into consideration," but the real meaning is more likely to be, "We shall take your proposal under advisement," i.e., "thanks but no thanks." Similarly *maemuki ni zensho (kentō) shimasu* "we shall deal with it (look into it) in a positive manner" should not be taken too literally.

## • *To omowanai ka?* Coaxing rather than coercing

Rather than sitting a listener down and telling her "how it is" or "how it's going to be," it is more polite to try to draw out her opinion even while you give your own. Rather than phrasing a statement as ~ *to omou/omoimasu*, it almost always sounds softer if you ask ~ *to omowanai/omoimasen ka*. And needless to say, requests couched as questions, rather than commands, are more polite.

These are ways to ask, in increasing levels of politeness, people for things or favors:

| TJ | TJ/NJ | NJ |
|---|---|---|
| ~ *(-te) kure* | | ~ *(-te) kudasai* |
| ~ *(-te) kureru?* | ~ *(-te) kudasaru? (F)* | ~ *(-te)kudasaimasu ka?* |
| ~ *(-te) kurenai?* | ~ *(-te) kudasaranai? (F)* | ~ *(-te) kudasaimasen ka?* |

## • *Hā* in NJ

The meanings and functions of *hā* depend on context and intonation. (1) Pronounced crisply and matter-of-factly, the shortened *ha* is used by subordinates in response to questions, requests or comments made by superiors. (2) A longer, drawn-out pronunciation suggests some uncertainty, doubt or suspicion. (3) A dramatically rising tone, like that sometimes heard in questions (*ha-a-A-A?*), expresses surprise.

(1) 君はロンドンに住んでいたことがあるんだってね。(TJ/M)
*Kimi wa Rondon ni sunde ita koto ga aru n' datte ne.*
Say, you've lived in London, I hear.
はあ、3年ほどですが……。(NJ/MF)
*Hā, san-nen hodo desu ga …*
Yes, sir, about three years, actually …

外出中に電話があったら、先方の名前と電話番号をメモして
　おいてください。(NJ/MF)
*Gaishutsu-chū ni denwa ga attara, senpō no namae to denwa-*
　*bangō o memo shite oite kudasai.*
Should there be any phone calls while I'm out, please be sure
　to get the person's name and telephone number.
はあ、承知しました。(NJ/MF)
*Hā, shōchi shimashita.*
Yes, sir (ma'am), I will.

(2) きょう、彼女会社を休んでいるんだってね。(TJ/MF)
*Kyō, kanojo kaisha o yasunde iru n' datte ne.*
She seems to have taken the day off.
はあ。(TJ/MF)
*Hā.*
Oh?

あいにく担当者が外出しておりまして、わかりかねますが……。
　(NJ/MF)
*Ainiku tantō-sha ga gaishutsu shite orimashite, wakari-kane-*
　*masu ga …*
Unfortunately the person in charge is out, and I'm afraid I am
　not familiar with the matter …
はあ。そうですか。(NJ/MF)
*Hā. Sō desu ka.*
Oh, I see.

(3) 彼女、今月末で退職されるそうです。(NJ/MF)
*Kanojo, kongetsu-matsu de taishoku sareru sō desu.*
I hear she's going to be quitting at the end of the month.
はあ？どうしてですか。(NJ/MF)
*Hā? Dō shite desu ka.*
Really? But why?

あの店は、去年つぶれました。(NJ/MF)

*Ano mise wa, kyonen tsuburemashita.*
That shop went out of business last year.
はあ？本当ですか。(NJ/MF)
*Hā? Hontō desu ka.*
What? Really?


## EQUIVALENCY CHART

| T-SHIRT JAPANESE | NECKTIE JAPANESE |
| --- | --- |
| *Konaida no* | *Rei no\** |
| *~ da kedo ne.* | *~ nan da kedo ne.†* |
| *dō ka na,* | *dō ka nē,†* |
| *… to iu to?* | *… to osshaimasu to?* |
| *Muri da* | *Chotto muzukashii* |
| *~ to omou yo.* | *~ to omowanai ka?†* |
| *~ ka na.* (M) | *~ deshō ka.* |
| *kotowatta* | *hakkiri sasete oita* |
| *ii darō* | *ii n' ja nai ka ne.†* |
| *~ kamo na.* | *~ kamo shiremasen ne.* |
| *Mukō* | *Senpō* |
| *ii n' ja nai ka na.* (M) | *tasukaru n' ja nai ka to omou kedo ne.†* |
| *Mā ne.* | *Hā.* |
| *Jā* | *De wa* |
| *sō suru ka.* | *sassoku sono hōkō de kentō itashimasu.* |

\* politely vague
† language used in Necktie conversations by a superior speaking to a subordinate